KEEPING THE BALANCE:

A Psychologist's Story

by

George W. Fairweather

Front cover artwork by:
    Robert A. Fairweather
    Petrouchka, 1993
    Charcoal and pencil drawing
    21 ¼" x 11 ⅜"

ISBN Number 0-9641068-2-5

Printed in the United States of America
at Morgan Printing in Austin, Texas

*This book is dedicated
to my wife, Betty J. Fairweather,
in recognition of her love,
help, support and tolerance.*

Preface

This book presents the true story of a psychologist who has attempted to improve the quality of life of the mentally ill. It is a story filled with feelings of both happiness and despair. All of the events depicted here actually happened to the author and/or his colleagues in the process of attempting to establish a meaningful role for the long-term mentally ill in the community. The scientific researches and their findings have been presented in numerous articles and books and are summarized in the recent book, *Empowering the Mentally Ill* by Fairweather and Fergus. This book presents the untold story of the thoughts and processes that took place on the personal side of this effort. It is an attempt to give the reader a more intimate account of the experiences of one person who spent the better part of his professional career trying to improve the interpersonal relationships and social status of the mentally ill. Some of the experiences of the professionals involved have been condensed or modified in order to make the account more readable. It is the author's hope that this story will make the public more aware of the problems of the mentally ill and the organizational and personal change that solutions to their social position require.

On a broader scale, the book is intended to demonstrate the pathway citizens must take to change outmoded social programs. To protect people, projects and institutions, names have been changed and no direct references have been made.

George W. Fairweather
Austin, Texas

Contents

CHAPTER 1
Learning to Learn

The war was over . . . the war was over . . . the war was over . . . . As I looked at our planes sitting quietly on the flight line, I thought that there must be some mistake. For months we flew over enemy territory every night in what seemed to me to be a pattern of living and dying that never changed. Being the closest squadron to Japan, we had heard rumors for weeks about the end of the war because of a new weapon, but we never thought it was true—especially since every time we heard a rumor that the war would end it didn't. So when it actually did, we didn't believe it. As I stood looking at the planes with the sand blowing in my face from the nearby beach of the island, I began to reflect on what had happened to me in this four and one-half years of what seemed like a dream. It couldn't have happened to me could it? Was this person with his flight suit, knife, revolver, bail-out bag and other accouterments really me—that peace-loving, married man who had such a supportive and loving wife. How could she ever know . . . how could anyone who hadn't lived through it ever know or understand the psychotic processes of a war that turned people who appeared to be kind and thoughtful into daily killers. What had happened to me? Was it that easy to turn a so-called normal individual into a messenger of death? Who were these people and these social forces that were so powerful that an entire society was willing to die for them? Or was it that underneath our facade we were all killers anyway . . . that our hostility and desire to control others was so much a part of us that we were unable to perceive that basically we were still "wild animals" not too dissimilar from the carnivorous lions and the like . . . loving and kind in one situation like mothers protecting their young, and ferocious killers in others when another animal invades our living area.

And then I thought of all those who had died. Was it really necessary? Were we going to have everlasting peace or was this just another war in a series of wars that might never end? What about those who died—their young wives and families? Did anyone care? What could be done to help them? Could they understand war? I couldn't. My thoughts were that there were no heroes, just ordinary people who suddenly found themselves in a psychotic world so brutal and lethal that constructive thought and loving behavior were completely subordinated to hostile and destructive behavior. And I hoped I would never hear again the voices that said, "This is what you will do. There is no alternative." I thought that I must have become an automated machine that simply lost emotional feeling in this horror called war.

And then my thoughts turned to those other victims of the war who had not been able to develop this machine like quality. Who couldn't make the transition from civilian life to being warriors. I thought particularly of my flying buddy, Andy. The last time I had seen him several weeks ago he had entered my tent and said he wanted to talk to me.

"Fine," I said, "Go ahead."

"Well," he responded, "I'm going to have to kill the doc."

"What are you talking about?" I replied.

"Well, I can't fly anymore—I just can't. It makes me feel so bad that I can't do it. You know the other night when I had to bail out for the second time and I landed behind enemy lines, I was almost killed several times by their guns. I went up again as soon as I reached the base because the commanding officer wanted me to fly immediately. I did fly but I almost wasn't able to land. I was shaking all over. I'm on my third tour of duty and you know how tough it's been. I just can't get into my fighter right now. I explained all this to the doc and he told me there was nothing wrong with me. I told him I wasn't going to fly anymore right now and maybe never again and he said, 'Oh, yes you are, there is nothing wrong with you.' I don't have any alternative . . . I'll just have to kill him and then he can't order me to fly. Will you go with me over to his tent so I can shoot him," he said, as he pulled his gun from its holster.

I began to try to convince him that his ideas were no solution to his problem, but I soon understood that he was going with or without me. And so I went.

As we entered the tent he looked at Dr. Rose and said, "I told you I couldn't fly anymore because I was sick. You said I wasn't sick and that I had to fly anyway. That it was all in my head."

As he raised the gun I grabbed it and took it away from him. Both Doctor Rose and I wrestled him to the ground and called for help. In a few days Andy was sent back to the States. When I walked from the infirmary with him to the plane he left on, I asked him about our earlier visit to Dr. Rose's tent.

Andy said, "I never saw Dr. Rose with you . . . you better go have your memory checked." As he climbed into the plane, he waved to me and yelled, "I'm sure glad I'm going home."

I thought about his memory loss—was it true he couldn't remember our walk to Dr. Rose's tent? If so, why? And then I wondered where he was now.

Upon returning to my tent, I met an old friend who had traveled to our island from another close by. In the course of our conversation we discussed what we might do in the future.

"You know, Bill," he said to me, "I think I know you pretty well and I think you ought to be an industrial engineer. You are good in math and you like people. It seems to me that would be an excellent choice. Since you've had no college why don't you try my engineering school in the Midwest?"

And so began a long discussion of an engineering career and the Midwestern University. That evening I wrote to my wife and asked her to send my records to the school. Shortly thereafter I was on a boat for home and entering college.

From the hot and humid climate of the South Pacific to the cold and snows of the Midwest was quite an adjustment in itself. But my lovely young wife helped me at every turn of the road, and, indeed, she has always been and remains today my chief supporter, friend and lover. Because of her love and support and willingness to work so we could survive, I was able to devote my entire time to getting an education. In addition, and of equal or greater importance, she was the one whose judgment I sought when academic or real life issues arose. She was then and is now a loving and helpful partner.

To me an education was far more than attending lectures. It was, in fact, an unrelenting search to try to understand the human condition. What did the interpersonal relationship, social, economic, biological, and religious experiences, among others, have to do with how we behaved and reacted to one another? How could we create better more humane societies? Could people eliminate war or were we hopelessly entrapped by out biological heritage? Because of these concerns, my interests soon turned away from the impersonal precision of thought required by engineering to the more person oriented humanities, social sciences, and natural sciences. Even so, my interest in mathematics continued and was transferred to the field of statistics.

As probably is true of all serious students, there are a few teachers who make a strong impact upon an individual. Since my interest in mathematics was very pronounced and my grades were excellent, I was permitted to take advanced courses from an internationally known statistician. I began to understand very quickly that we seemed to be on the same logical wavelength. From the very outset of the courses he emphasized that statistics were tools to be used to improve scientific knowledge and were not an end in themselves. All of his examples were attempts to show us that if we applied statistics properly we could use them to help solve human problems. And he constantly emphasized that to do this one must not only be a good statistician, but also must be an expert in the field in which s/he did research. His own field was agronomy and he often showed us the fields where research was taking place and told us how the crop yields would be compared in order that farmers could improve their practices. An offhand remark that he made to a student one day impressed me then and does so even to this day. The student said he wanted to be a great agronomist.

"What," he asked the professor, "should be the first thing I do to enhance my chances?"

The professor said, "First, learn to drive a tractor."

The student continued, "No, I mean what statistical courses should I take?"

The professor continued, "First learn to drive a tractor—if you can't do that and are the world's greatest statistician, you still won't understand what happens in the field and therefore you can't understand and interpret whatever you have found." Then he added, "Of course, this is not the most glamorous side of the career so many people become excellent statisticians but poor scientists."

Many of my own experiences later on were to reflect the truth of this statement. But there were experiences outside the classroom that constantly reminded me that many of the students were veterans. Because of the massive number of veterans that had descended upon the school, my wife and I found temporary housing in a house owned by an elderly couple who were trying to help the incoming veterans by renting rooms to married couples. We took turns doing the kitchen chores and one night one of the other couples had an argument. Jake picked up a knife, and as my wife and I watched, he threw it into the wall where it was buried to the hilt?

"What in the hell are you doing?" I asked.

He responded, "Well, I was a *kriege* (German war prisoner) for two years. It's a hangover from my days in the prison camp. We used to get so angry that we weren't rescued and were so mistreated that we all learned to throw those knives very well. We often wished we could throw them at our captors but they stood there with guns on us so we couldn't. I just got so angry at Ellen—she yelled at me—that without a thought I threw the knife. It was exactly the feeling I got in the prison camp. There was no thought—I just did it automatically. I'll try not to do it again, but its so much a part of me I can't be sure." I was later to learn about post-war trauma and its lasting effects.

Soon after that experience, my wife and I leased an apartment on a farm. We often wondered what happened to the *"kriege."*

Other experiences reminded me that we were an older more serious group than the younger students. In one class a young student asked two of us (both veterans) if we wanted to buy a copy of a test we were soon to be given.

The fellow standing next to me said, "Where did you get this test?"

The younger person said, "From one of my fraternity brothers; we frequently get tests."

The veteran grabbed the test and tore it up and

said, "I'm going to tell the professor about this and you better tell your fraternity brothers to stop this practice. We're serious students and we don't like people cheating on us." And there were other experiences that were humorous. In one advanced math class one of the younger students who had not studied for the test wrote down for every answer, "God alone knows." When he received the examination back the professor had given him a grade of 100. When he opened the paper, the professor had written, "God alone gets the credit— you don't." When he showed me the paper, we both laughed and he said, "Well, the old guy sure has a sense of humor." There were other humorous events such as the time a group of veterans decided they would help me and my young wife paper our apartment. When I was not looking, they poured beer into the paste for the wallpaper. After they left and we went to bed, all we could hear all night long was "pop, pop, pop," as the wallpaper burst from the expanding yeast in the beer. Needless to say, they were never invited to help us with any other jobs.

School continued to be very interesting and challenging. What became clearer to me with every new bit of information gained from the classes was how interrelated all the different so-called sciences and humanities were. This seemed all the more evident since no such divisions existed in the real world. It appeared clear to me that to solve human problems of any importance one had to consider all the fields at once because problems occurred in the real world not in the laboratory. The natural sciences, social sciences and the humanities were different ways of looking at the same phenomenon. This led me to wonder how universities ever divided the natural world into so many diverse categories. Eventually, it occurred to me that this had happened over time as a means of controlling the social and political power of the universities. Thus, one could develop a field of study—declare it different from any other field—and establish her/his own budget, procedures, and political power. In such a way, the economic and political power of individuals and groups was established and maintained. At least something like this must have happened since humans have such a need to control others—a matter that was already obvious to me from life in general and particularly from my war experiences.

As time went on I drifted toward the field of psychology since the general interest there seemed to be one of attempting to understand human perception and behavior. It was also an historical moment when the field's boundaries were not set in stone. In those days, one could even ask, "What is psychology?" and get numerous different answers depending upon who one asked. But there was a unanimity of opinion that it was and must continue to be a science. Since its borders overlapped with so many other fields, I felt more at home there rather than in the more well-defined and boundary protected fields.

One course that was particularly interesting to me was that of Abnormal Psychology. While I had no experience with mental illness as such, except with Andy, (the *kriege*), and the unusual experiences with the everyday behavior of some maladjusted persons in combat, I had seen many who wept openly and some who finally became immobile and could not walk or eat. There were a few who carried out extensive conversations with people who weren't there and some who believed that the enemy was in their tent when no one was there. I was later to learn that these were symptoms of mental illness. But at that time I simply knew that these behaviors were odd and that they often appeared to be completely irrational. And even though I had no formal training about mental illness as such I also had a wealth of experiences with the odd behavior of "normal" persons that I was later to discover were sometimes symptoms of mental illness. I thought maybe I could find out more about such problems. Some of the personality theories seemed to be relevant, but I was most persuaded of the need for treatment program research by a day's visit to a "home for the mentally retarded."

One of the field trips in our course took us to this home. As I entered the first building, I was told that the most retarded individuals in the institution resided here. My introduction came as a shock. Here grown persons were crawling on the floor with diapers on and making grunting noises. As I watched them crawl around I became more and more depressed and then angry. I asked the professor who accompanied us if there was not some way of improving their lives. Some program in which these people could participate.

"No," he told me, "this is the best program we have. They can't learn anything. They can't even learn to take care of themselves, including keeping themselves clean."

As the day went on I became more and more disgusted with the way in which these persons were treated even those who were said to be only marginally retarded. Since my own life experiences led me to believe that the environment in which people find themselves greatly influences how they react, I did not accept the professor's negativism. Certainly, I thought, we should be able to do better than this. It occurred to me that this was an "out of sight, out of mind solution." Later I asked the institution's director if any research was being conducted with regard to their ability to adjust in this institutional environment.

"I don't know of any," he responded, "of course you have to find some interested scientists and get them some research money. I know of neither. It's not hard to get scientists and money for biological research in the laboratory but research in institutions like this is almost unheard of—no one wants to do that kind of research. They might get their hands dirty. But research in a nice clean laboratory leading to scientific publications and salary increases is the way to go for a career-oriented scientist. And don't think young scientist's don't know that."

"They should be required to take a course from my statistics professor and they would learn that unless you know the day-to-day experiences of people you can't understand their problems much less find a solutions to them," I retorted.

"I would agree with that," said the director, "and believe me, I don't like this any more than you do. But I have no money of my own, so I'm stuck with the institutional practices."

On my way home, I thought, *this has not been a good day for me personally, but I've learned a lot even if it is only that institutions don't change readily if at all.*

Toward the end of my junior year, the head of the psychology department called me into his office and asked me what I was going to do after graduation.

I answered, "I don't know. I haven't given it much thought."

Then he said, "I really think you should consider going to graduate school in Psychology to get an advanced degree in this field."

Following this discussion, I had several conversations with friends and family, and at the beginning of my senior year I decided that I would apply to graduate school in Psychology. Almost immediately I was asked if I was willing to be interviewed about entry into graduate school, and I, of course, said I would be happy to talk with anyone about their school. Shortly thereafter, I was informed that a well-known psychologist was coming to the campus and I was given a date for the interview. I had one suit and a pair of dress boots left over from my days in the air force and so one morning I put on my best dress clothes and left for the interview. I was introduced to the professor and ushered into a room where the interview took place.

After some banter about innocuous topics, the interviewer said, "Why did you wear those boots today?"

What a strange question, I thought, but I then answered, "They are the only pair of dress shoes I have."

"Well," he said, "it's a shame that you would come to such an important meeting with boots on."

"They were good enough for me while I was defending this country," I shot back.

He continued, "Are you married?"

"Yes," I replied.

"How old were you and your wife when you got married?" he asked.

"I was twenty-two and she was eighteen," I answered.

"That was far too young to get married," he stated.

At that point, I stood up and said, "I'm sorry,

but I have better things to do. I am not interested in your school."

As I walked toward the door, he said, "Congratulations, you have just completed a stress interview and your handling of it was right on track."

"You must not have heard me," I repeated, "I am not interested in your school, and if you are as interested in stress, as you say, you ought to look up my combat record in the service."

When I arrived home, I told my wife Betty about the so-called stress interview and I remarked, "I hope his approach is not symptomatic of the field of psychology—if it is, I'm going to do something else. I'm not interested in making people feel uncomfortable."

Shortly thereafter, I was asked to come for an interview with one of the leading psychologists in the country. To get there my wife and I drove all day and we got a motel room for the night so that I could meet the psychologist for an early morning interview. When I got to the psychologist's office, I went up to his secretary and said I had arrived for the interview.

She looked at me and smiled and said, "And you're right on time. I'll tell the professor you're here."

There was glass between the secretary's office and the professor and I noticed he was reading when she announced that I was waiting for the interview. She returned and added, "Professor

Helms will be with you in a minute so why don't you have a seat."

After sitting for an hour, I got up and asked her, "Do you think I could see the professor now?".

She said she would ask him again and disappeared into his office. She soon returned and mumbled, "I am embarrassed that he will not see you since you came so far at his invitation. He wants you to come back tomorrow since he is absorbed in his reading."

"No," I retorted, "I'll not be back."

When I returned to the motel and told my wife, she said, "Maybe there is something wrong with the people in this field."

As we left the motel for our trip home, I said to her, "Maybe you are right. Maybe there is something wrong with these people. They seem to think they're God. I hope this isn't what we fought the war to save."

When we arrived home, a telegram was waiting which informed me that I had been admitted to a well-known university with a stipend in the new field of "clinical psychology." I called the University to see if I needed to have an interview.

"No, your record speaks for itself." I was told.

I turned to Betty and said, "Amazing. Someone read the material I sent and really didn't care what I looked like. I think we should go there." And we did.

CHAPTER 2
Is This Science or What?

Since I had no intention of becoming involved in the field of mental illness prior to graduating from the University, my background in its origins and treatment was very limited. It was in this naive context that my journey into professional psychology began. Since I had a strong background in statistics and in scientific methodology I thought that my role in the field would be that of a researcher. But I also knew from my scientific training that such a role would require "hands-on" experience with the mentally ill. As my statistics professor had told me, "Your interpretation of any research finding will depend upon a thorough knowledge of the problem you are investigating."

Shortly after arriving at the university for graduate training I received my introduction to the field of mental illness. All of the new class members soon learned the diagnostic nomenclature and the existing theories of mental illness. And we began attending diagnostic sessions. In these sessions numerous professionals presented what their interviews, life histories, psychological tests and medical techniques showed the diagnosis to be. Collating all of this information the senior psychiatrist arrived at a diagnosis. Following the lengthy diagnosis, treatment was prescribed. Strangely enough only four treatments were available other than the typical medications—electric shock therapy, insulin shock therapy, psychotherapy and work. It seemed a little strange to me that we were spending so much time in minute diagnostic processes when we essentially only had four treatments. And then one day the students were introduced to the therapies.

My first reaction to viewing electric shock therapy was that of surprise and concern. While I was a veteran with a great deal of combat experience I had rarely seen a body bounce around like the patients' did when the current was introduced into their bodies. In another large room a number of very obese patients who were receiving insulin shock treatment sat around. They were very lethargic and rarely moved. When I tried to talk to them they often said nothing or only a few words. I turned to one of the professional persons giving the treatment and said, "Is this treatment really effective?"

"Of course," he said, "Why else would we give it?"

Why else indeed, I thought. But the visions of those bouncing bodies and the obese silent ones would be remembered from that day forward.

With these experiences as background my interest in psychotherapy became enhanced. Perhaps this was the treatment program that I would find most helpful. With this in mind, I began my psychotherapy training. As I sat through the many hours of lectures and endless readings it became clear to me that mental illness—even from a theoretical perspective—was simply "normal" human behavior that was outside what is culturally accepted perception and behavior. It involved an individual's attempt to adjust to levels of high anxiety and feelings of being unaccepted—the same adjustmental techniques that Andy had exhibited with the flight surgeon. Furthermore, it appeared that heredity and learning were both part of the equation that led to neurotic and psychotic behavior. Different theories about the origins of mental illness emphasized the interpersonal and social environment and/or biological processes rooted in heredity as the central causes of mental illness. Thus, in the final analysis, one had to consider life's experiences, the culture in which one lived, the person's biological processes, and numerous other variables. And with my scientific training, I was constantly surprised at the dogmatism with which persons with different theoretical positions viewed their chosen theory. This position is perhaps best summarized in the statement of a neurologist who met me in the hall one day and voiced his opposition to psychological theory.

"Why do you reject the idea of the possible effectiveness of psychotherapeutic treatments?" I asked.

"Because the problem is all in the brain," he said. Then he added with a grin, "Do you know the difference between psychology and bullshit?"

"No," I answered.

"Bullshit has some utility—you can use it for manure," he said with a grin.

Despite these statements, my interest in psychotherapeutic treatments continued.

Various psychotherapeutic treatments were based upon different theoretical notions—psychoanalysis on unconscious conflicts based on repressed sexual drives as the origin of conflict; other theories concerned other conflicts such as the lack of identity and feelings of inferiority: others were based upon anxiety and conflict over what one should be, and so on. All claimed success by resolving these conflicts through perceptual changes that led to improved self-concept and its associated behavioral change. And to make matters more complicated, tranquilizing medication was introduced about this time. Observation showed that at least in the hospital situation overly aggressive behavior and some other psychotic symptoms were alleviated through their use.

The different personality theorists were treated as celebrities with their own group of disciples who argued long and hard for their point of view. As a youngster, I had spent a good deal of time with church groups and it seemed to me that despite all my scientific training, I was back in a religious setting. Each theoretical school seemed to be superimposing theoretical notions on every individual's perceptions and behaviors without a great deal of scientific evidence from unbiased sources that any of them explained sufficiently human activities and relations. Recalling the words of the nationally known statistician with whom I had studied earlier—"without scientific evidence that one theoretical notion is more predictive than any other, accept any one you choose because in such cases they are all the same anyway."

As my training progressed, I began to be more and more puzzled by the claims of "cure" by all of the different theorists. The supporters of each theoretical position, however, seemed to have little scientific evidence that their theories were correct, indeed that their application resulted in any more successful patient adjustment than any other. In many ways each theory seemed to have a group of believers much like a religious group. My scientific training made me wonder about the theories and their claimed results.

About this time, I attended a psychotherapy seminar where a world renowned psychotherapist was showing his audience the value of his techniques. We sat in an auditorium as different patients were brought in one by one and interviewed while displaying their symptoms. The diagnosis of each was described and revealed to the audience of professionals as if the patients were not there. I felt depressed watching this "show" and became more concerned than I had been about the typical professional role. Often, after the patient left there was laughter. I wondered about how the patient must feel being treated like a show horse or a show dog. Then finally the psychotherapist entered with a mute patient and began his procedures. He strutted around the stage and yelled at the patient with some choice theoretical notions about his problems and his relationships with his parents. Finally, the patient spoke some unintelligible words and shortly thereafter was led off the stage. The therapist then lectured to us about the patient's progress in this first meeting. I left feeling that we had been watching a narcissistic display by the psychotherapist at the expense of the patient. Even though my own training continued, I began to wonder more and more about whether the treatments were valid or a myth growing out of accepted belief systems.

This concern about the validity of the treatments we were giving the patients became more goal-oriented one day as I read about mental illness and science simultaneously. I found myself reading over and over one article by an internationally known scientist in which the scientist said that what practitioners had forgotten was how to say "I don't know."

One day after reading this article I got into the elevator in the library with a distinguished sociologist from whom I was taking a course. He turned to me and said, "What is this I hear about psychologists wanting to be licensed?."

"I have heard the same things from my colleagues," I replied.

"That's a shame," he responded.

"Why?" I asked.

"Well," he replied, "once one is licensed it means that you are dealing with the past. The assumption is made that this relatively new field has accumulated enough knowledge so that this knowledge can be administered to the public with a great deal of confidence. Licensing essentially requires the end of scientific thought in the psychology of mental health because no one would be licensed to practice new helpful programs as they are found. Those already in practice often perceive new programs as threatening their livelihood since they know nothing about them."

"Why can't new programs be accepted into the field when they have been demonstrated to be effective?" I inquired.

The sociologist answered, "Not in psychology since it is behavioral science, that is it often requires changing the role of the psychologist and sometimes the entire system and educational processes. Where by contrast in medicine one often does not change the role only the pills or the techniques." The truth of this statement was to occur to me over and over again in my career.

About the same time, my training psychotherapist asked me to be very careful in treating the mentally ill because the therapist is often in a very powerful position with the patient. He told me of a famous musician treated by a fellow psychoanalyst who cured the patient, but in the process the patient gave up his music.

"I wonder," he mused, "what the musician and the world were deprived of by the cure."

And the same day, another psychoanalyst said to me, "Do not talk to patients about their lives before three years of age until you have completed a psychoanalysis."

"Why?" I asked.

"Because you don't know enough," he quipped.

All of these discussions and many others made me more concerned about what treatments helped people and in what ways. And so at this point I decided to do some studies of my own in an attempt to see what I could discover.

I began by observing and talking to those patients who came back to the hospital after treatment. I interviewed every one that I could who returned to the hospital and I began comparing their statements with those of patient improvement by their therapists shown in their charts when they left. In most cases the patient was considered to have resolved unconscious conflicts by their treatment specialist and to have the proper medication upon leaving the hospital. But over and over I was told an entirely different story by the returnee. The following was a typical reaction

"Doc, my other doctor wanted me to talk about my family and fears and anxieties I had . . . and I did. I felt good when I left, but upon a return to my family I went back to the company for whom I worked. I was told that I had been terminated. I looked for work every day but I was always told there were no jobs. Finally, one personnel manager told me that I might as well quit looking for work because I had spent time in a mental hospital. I got all nervous again and I couldn't do anything at all so I came back here. I didn't know what else to do."

At this point, I would examine the patient's file and it usually stated that, at the time he left, he had indeed recovered and was ready to resume his work and community life. Other interviews with returnees gave much the same information. After compiling a great deal of information that showed a clear pattern of rejection by community members—particularly employers—I began to discuss this problem with others.

After showing the information to a psychiatrist friend of mine, he said, "Bill, I believe your information is entirely correct. But we have no employment program in the community and are limited to what we can do for the people here in the hospital which clearly has to be to change the individual. So these people will participate in our therapy programs because they are the only ones we have."

"Well, John," I responded, "maybe we should create some new roles that would deal with these community rejections that appear to be central to these people's community adjustment."

He responded, "You're talking about changing an entire system of theory and practice. If you can do it, good luck to you. I applaud you, but I'm a physician not an agent of social change."

I began to think about what all of this meant. Of course, Maslow's research implied that there was little use in trying to change the thought processes until people have met their basic survival needs—housing, food and the like because those thoughts aimed at survival require all of one's creative energy. About that time there were also several sociologists writing who talked about the detrimental effects of incarceration. So I decided to look into related problems with criminals who were incarcerated. At that time the literature was replete with statements that chronic criminals could not learn, so I decided to do some research into their ability to learn. Many theorists believed that the criminal psychopath could not learn to be socialized and therefore had to be forever incarcerated. These ideas afforded me the opportunity to study the effects of long-term incarceration. So with my wife and baby son, I traveled to a prison filled with long-term criminals to conduct the study.

When I arrived, I was ushered into the warden's office. He told me of the dangers I would encounter in the prison and told me the security staff would make it as safe for me as they could. We had many talks after that in which he told me of his problems in the prison not the least of which was his concern that incarceration might, in fact, lead to more criminal behavior particularly since once the criminals left the prison they were often rejected by society and, most important, could not find employment or any meaningful social role. In our discussions he pointed out that the problem was not a question of their ability to work since many were foremen in the prison with excellent work records but rather a problem of social rejection by others. And my own learning research seemed to bear out his concerns. In fact, my research in learning showed that even the most hardened criminals could learn new concepts if they were motivated to do so. After my research in the learning processes of criminals I returned to the University to complete my dissertation and to receive my doctorate in psychology.

But I was again to encounter the egocentric and authoritarian role of some of my fellow professionals. When I had finished my doctoral research in the learning processes of criminals my advisor called me into his office one day. He began, "I think you have done an excellent piece of research in learning and it should be published in a research journal. Why don't you rewrite it for a journal article and send it to Dr. Williams who, as you know, is one of the most respected learning researchers in the country."

"That sounds like a good idea to me except that some of my findings do not support his theoretical ideas," I responded.

"Oh, he's a broad thinker," my advisor replied, "and would most certainly change his ideas when new evidence is presented."

And so I spent several days rewriting the research so it met the journal requirements. A few weeks later my article was returned to me by Dr. Williams with an attached letter. It stated that the article would be accepted for publication if I made a number of corrections. A brief review of the list of corrections that had to be made showed that they all were aimed at eliminating findings that questioned his theoretical notions.

When I saw my advisor later and showed him the letter he said, "Well, now you have had your introduction to the politics of science." Needless to say, the research was never resubmitted for publication but it did serve to direct most of my future publications to books where I could publish the scientific information in its entirety. It also soured my interest in science since after many discussions with other scientists I found that they often had ideas to defend or promote that helped them select the "correct" articles to publish. It led me to state to a close friend, "Is this science or what?"

This experience entered into my decision to turn down academic positions in favor of clinical work. And so I accepted a position as a clinical psychologist with a large hospital in a southwestern state. When I arrived on the grounds I was sent to the director's office. "I am certainly happy to see you, he said, because we want you to work on our national tuberculosis research project."

"But I accepted this position with the agreement that I would do no research—only service work with mentally ill patients," I responded.

He replied, "Well, since you accepted the job, we have received this large grant to study the effects of long-term hospitalization upon tubercular patients. Your background in scientific methodology and your experience with incarcerated criminals makes you a perfect candidate for the job. I have, however, freed up some of your time for diagnostic and therapeutic work with the mentally ill."

"Well, I guess I can live with that," I responded. And so began my first service and research job.

After meeting the research staff, I began seeing and interviewing the tuberculosis patients. The effects of long-term hospitalization soon became evident in the constant anger and depression of many of the patients. Most of them longed to go home and resume their lives. However, this was not permitted while they could infect someone else. Our studies began to show some additional problems with confinement particularly with highly active goal-oriented individuals—their death rate was high. One of the research physicians became extremely interested in these findings and his biochemical studies showed rapid chemical changes in the most physically and mentally active patients. And so he decided to try some home treatments with these persons by training them and their families in appropriate techniques to prevent transmission of the disease. An almost immediate improvement in these patients ensued. And so the home treatment of tubercular patients began at least in this hospital. Others would soon follow.

But I also kept seeing mentally ill patients in psychotherapy. Influenced by my earlier studies of high return rates among certain patients and my research experience with tubercular patients I began again to follow-up patients upon discharge from the hospital. Again I found the difficulty many of them had in getting their jobs back and in leading a meaningful life in the community. It seemed that their diagnoses of mental illness were as much a deterrent to adequate community life as was the illness itself. It was at this juncture in my life that I was offered an opportunity to develop a research project that would address this issue. And so we moved to the East Coast for a service-research position in a large psychiatric hospital.

CHAPTER 3

The Search Begins: The Marriage of Science and Practice

What had become evident by this time was several factors that would influence my future life's work. First it seemed to me that mental illness had many facets—economic, political, biological, psychological, geographical, religious and others. In addition it seemed clear to me that scientific research should be used to solve these problems if scientists and practitioners alike were to adopt the position that scientific evidence should be used to improve the human condition. This became an issue with me because I was reading widely of Einstein's concern about the egocentric nature of some of his scientific colleagues as well as his attempt to understand why people had such a strong drive to control others—this growing out of his experiences in Nazi Germany. I was also impressed by the fact that it was not until Oppenheimer, his student, observed the first atomic explosion in New Mexico that Oppenheimer reportedly said, "Something must be done about this." What this meant to me was that the notion that science could be used to improve or destroy human beings had not been an issue to the physicists until the destructive potential of their discoveries had become so obvious that it could no longer be denied.

The need to use science humanely became even more of an issue with me after discussing it with a physicist friend of mine. He was an outstanding young physicist but seemed oblivious to any responsibility he or other physicists might have for the use of their findings. When I asked him a simple question, "What do you believe the social responsibility of the physicist is—especially given the development of the bomb?" He replied, "I know nothing about that. I didn't take any courses in my training about that."

"But don't you think since you and your colleagues are now dealing with forces that could blow up the world that someone familiar with this research should at least be involved in discussing its possible consequences?" I asked.

He responded, "You have to realize that most physicists are like little kids playing with erector sets . . . they want to build whatever interests them. Social consequences are not considered—at least as far as I know."

"From this time on, I'm going to try to make a special issue of how science can be used to improve the human condition," I asserted.

"What do you mean by that?" he asked.

"Well, I'm going to try to use scientific methods to help solve human problems; but the only solutions that I will consider are those that are humane and are aimed at improving the human condition." As I walked away I thought, *Hopefully, I can use scientific findings to improve the plight of the mentally ill.*

This was my overriding concern when I began my research on the value of different treatment techniques in 1955. I had heard my colleagues tell about their treatment successes over and over again. At the same time I spent endless hours reading about the treatment techniques of the leading psychotherapy theorists. But what I could not find was any scientifically sound research that compared the different therapies on extensive follow-up of the clients. Furthermore, they all compared patients on different types of measures usually involving relations between the therapist and patient but with no evaluation of the patient outside of the therapy situation. At this point I decided that if I was to contribute to the life adjustment of the mentally ill it would be necessary to at least compare the most frequently used therapies with each other. In addition, it was also important that measures both inside and outside the therapy sessions took place to explore whether what happened in the therapy sessions was indeed related to the real life experiences of the patients. To accomplish this it was necessary to get the hospital's support for the study.

And so I designed an experiment to explore these ideas. But I was soon to find out that attempting to explore the cherished theories and practices of trained professionals was not an easy task.

When I told a close friend about my intentions he said, "Don't do it, Bill. You should know by now that these people want to practice what they've been trained to do."

I replied, "But they all also have had some scientific training which should have taught them to always question what they are doing?"

"Well," he answered, "they never took the scientific message seriously since they all knew that once licensed they didn't need it."

"Am I to assume that their sole interest is in making money through the use of beliefs that may have little or no scientific merit?" I inquired.

"Believe whatever you will," he responded, "But once you start you will find out that if your scientific results do not corroborate their pet theories their reaction will be to do everything they can to discredit your findings."

"Well, I guess that's the price of freedom," I replied.

I began first by collecting and looking systematically at the patients' current follow-up information. As I suspected, the results were the same as I had found earlier as a graduate student—seventy-five percent of those with previous hospitalizations returned to this hospital in six months after being declared "cured," or "much improved." At this point I talked to a colleague, David Dunn, about trying to find out what, if any, of our treatments worked and, if some did, with whom.

His response to me was, "Bill, you know better than anyone because of your experimental and statistical training that the only way we're ever going to find out is by conducting an experiment whose goal is to answer your questions. And for one, I think you ought to do what you think is right. Pay no attention to your peers because they all belong to one theoretical camp or another, and are thereby defendants of the status quo. So I'll support you because I think it's time we find out what treatments work and with whom. Or for that matter, maybe none of them work—and that we should know most of all."

With this advice and my own feeling that we ought to be able to do better for the mentally ill, I sat down to design an experiment that would shed as much light on treatment procedures and their successes or failures as I could. After many days and weeks, I went to see David. I showed him the design that compared four treatments—individual psychotherapy from several different theoretical points of view, group psychotherapy, a group living situation designed earlier by an internationally known psychiatrist, and work therapy. Volunteer patients with three different diagnoses—neurotics, acute psychotics, and long-term psychotics—were to be compared. These groups were to be compared over time on one hundred and twenty different measures. These evaluations were generally in the areas of personal feelings, perceptions, and behaviors before, during, and following treatment. After discussing this potential experiment with my colleagues and other friends I went before the research review panel with my proposal to try to get their approval to carry out the research.

After the presentation the panel almost immediately became divided into three groups. One group supported the research and cited the need for such information; a second group expressed the belief that we already knew enough about treatment effectiveness and therefore did not need it; and a third group thought it might result in too much questioning of different techniques. According to them, therapists had to believe in a theory in order to do therapy and the results might lead them to question their own theories and thus make them ineffective therapists. The arguments went on and on with various members taking one of the three positions just mentioned. Just when I thought we were in "gridlock" a distinguished professor from a major university who was also a well-known psychoanalyst asked to speak. He was well-respected by all the members so I listened intently. I also thought he might have a significant impact upon the group's decision.

"My friends," he started, "what Dr. Fairweather has proposed is something we should all support. In fact, I want to congratulate him and his colleagues for their attempt to increase our knowledge. And I might add it is much needed. Let me speak from my own experience gained through treatment of many patients over 30 years. I have had several who I have seen now for over twenty years. In my judgment they have not responded as well to psychoanalysis as some of my other patients have. I further believe that they come to me not so much to gain insight about their problems but more for my support and counsel about what to do about some everyday problems. I personally would like to find out if another program might be more effective for them and if so what it is. Even though as you all know I was trained and practice psychoanalysis that does not mean that there might not be a better therapy for some individuals nor does it mean that I have to be defensive about my theoretical position. The more knowledge we have the better off we will all be. Therefore I endorse this research completely and hope that everyone here will do likewise." The vote was then taken and the research was approved.

A few minutes after the vote and as we were leaving the room he asked to see me for a few minutes. "Bill," he said, "don't be distracted from your inquiry. I know many of the people here and some of them feel very threatened by your proposal. Suppose it should show that we need some new kind of program that they are not prepared to offer. So, regardless of what you find try to put yourself in their position and find a way to provide for them a new and more useful role. They're good people—just afraid of something new. You will find as you go along just how difficult change is for all human beings—you and me included. Good luck to you and if you need any further help, let me know." As he left I thought back to the few great teachers I had known and it was clear to me that he was another. With the panel's approval, the research soon began.

After endless hours the research staff, treatment staff, patients, and space were obtained. And then came the endless days of operating the program and measuring the results. All of the information was filed without being read until the last day of the study was completed. At this point the analysis of the data began.

As the analyses progressed, I looked at each and every sheet with fascination. I had no idea what to expect since all the data were collected and filed earlier. It soon became evident that a pattern of results was coming from the data. Generally, it appeared with as close to scientific certainty as one can get that the different treatments had the same effect over long periods of time. The different psychotherapies, which showed some early effects in real life adjustment, lost their advantage as time passed. By the end of eighteen months they showed no different results than work therapy. In addition, hospital behavior and perceptions did not transfer to the community giving a clear picture that whatever changes did occur in the hospital had little or no effect in community life. And behaviors and perceptions were not related, i.e.,—gaining insight into one's problems did not mean that the behavior of the person would change. Thus, the fact that one could understand the reasons for her/his behavior—overly aggressive behavior toward spouse, for example, did not mean that the behavior changed.

But the most notable result occurred with the different diagnostic groups. Eighty percent of all the acute psychotic patients showed sufficient improvement so that they did not need additional hospitalization. Fifty percent of the neurotic patients did not seek further treatment either. But seventy-five percent of the persons with a history of mental illness returned to the hospital during the first eighteen months after treatment. I immediately began discussing these findings with other professionals. Again the process resulted in three different reactions—we should do something about the community adjustment of the patients, particularly the long-termers; the findings would be different if only I were their therapist; and the research itself interfered with the outcomes. The data analyses and research results seemed to have little effect upon each professional person's view of their own treatment methods. One therapist summed it up best when he said, "Who cares what the results show. I know I'm a successful therapist."

But the results had affected me a great deal. The words of my old statistics professor kept ringing in my ears—"When you have done everything you can to evaluate accurately your experimental data and it still remains the same, then you should accept it as a fact and use it as a basis for theory building." I reviewed the experiment over and over—discussed the technicalities with friends, and finally decided that I must do something to improve our treatments, especially for the long-termers. But I knew now that to do so would make me a member in opposition to the majority. But as my friend David Dunn had told me earlier, "You have to do what you think is right." And so the long journey toward solving the problems of the long-term mentally ill began. At this point in history, I had no idea of the lessons that were in store for me.

CHAPTER 4
Discovering Problem-Solving Groups

Since all the results had indicated that many patients we saw daily in the hospital would remain there unless some new program was developed that would help them in their adjustment outside the hospital situation, I began to think of new approaches. The results of my researches kept repeating themselves over and over again. Simply put, patients who had been in the hospital for a number of months or years tended to return to the hospital at exceedingly high rates of about 75% in 18 months.

The reason for the returns again became obvious as I filtered through the research. Although they varied to some extent with each individual, the results were the same: these individuals were discriminated against because of their past hospitalization and psychiatric diagnoses. Few were able to find work and many of the families were unable to give them any help either in the work or housing situations. It was this lack of social position in the community and the lack of opportunity to succeed in any field of endeavor that became central in my thinking. Accordingly, I started some discussions about possible solutions with several interested friends.

My colleagues and I had one meeting after another attempting to come up with an innovative solution that might help these persons lead a more "normal" life in the community. While talking about the problem of the long-termers with a friend one day, he suddenly said, "Hell, these people have something in common with all minorities—they're living in a hostile environment. What you have to do is come up with some social system that protects them from this utter rejection . . . you know . . . circle the wagons."

And then I thought *Why not use group members to support each other?* Many studies had shown the strength of a motivated group. I was also familiar with the street gang studies that showed how they protected their members even though they had different social goals. These persons could become a real asset to their society. At the same time, a study was released about army troops that escaped from the enemy in Korea. That study showed that those soldiers who organized themselves into groups and whose goal was to return to Inchon as ordered by MacArthur often survived while those who decided to "go it alone" did not.

While discussing this with a historian friend of mine, he said, "Sure the small problem-solving group makes sense. In a way that's what the emigrants did. They lived next door to each other and provided support from those hostile persons with whom they worked. These persons often made fun of them because they spoke poor English and had strange habits. But the local group from the same country provided them support."

But my traditional psychology friends believed such an approach would not work. A close friend said, "They're so psychotic how can they make good judgments?"

"Well," I responded, maybe a few persons within the group can band together and make good judgments at a particular moment in time. We both know that these people have their ups and downs and there may be enough functioning persons at any one time to help them all, particularly if they want to live in the community."

He responded, "I think it will fail since they will have no insight into their problems and will therefore be unable to help anyone, even themselves."

"But almost all of them tell me that despite their problems they could do all right in the community if their basic survival needs—housing, food, a job—could be met. In any event, I'm going to try to study this aspect of their adjustment," I argued.

Convinced of the need for a new approach, the

first research step I had to take was to find out if these persons could, in fact, organize themselves into problem-solving groups. At that time I went to see a psychiatrist, Bob Morse, and told him of my concern and interests. Unlike many other professionals he said, "I think it's a great idea. I'm personally sick and tired of seeing these people come back to the hospital. Your research certainly fits into my experience. I'll help you try to do something new for these long-term patients. Nothing else seems to work so I like you feel obligated to see what we can do. I'll support you in your effort." And so my studies about small problem-solving groups began.

Since my thinking had led me to the conclusion that we would first have to organize small problem-solving groups to find out if they could solve their members' problems and help them survive in a hostile community environment, I asked a social psychologist to help me organize the groups and to help me create developmental processes from which we could generate such groups. From a number of my studies and the small group scientific literature we began studying group problem-solving with the mentally ill. We found some helpful group dynamics that can be summarized as follows: (1) Groups did not develop a willingness to adopt and work upon a common goal unless leadership came from within their own ranks. (2) They were only responsive to common everyday rewards such as money and free time, i.e., they would work as a group under conditions where there was a group and individual reward of money and free time for good performance. (3) Groups that could not develop good leadership did not do well but those who did surpassed our expectations. (4) Solving group and individual problems occurred when all members perceived the group as helpful to them and when the members believed they had a stake in the system. When all of these central conditions were present and proper training was available, groups could solve their members' problems.

Once having discovered the basic elements of creating problem-solving groups, I discussed all of our findings with the supportive psychiatrist, Bob Morse.

Since the results are clear, I said, "I think we should try to operate a hospital ward with these groups empowered to take all the responsibility we can legally give them in this setting and see how it affects their hospital and community adjustment."

Bob became very quiet at this point and replied, "I agree, but how? I think we can get hospital approval, but you know there are going to be those who will not agree and they might make it somewhat unpleasant for us. Let me talk to the director and others and we'll discuss it further later." A few days later he asked me to come into his office and announced, "We have the necessary support. Now you'll have to design the program and we'll discuss it further at that time."

"Fine," I replied, "I'll see you soon."

With the help of my colleagues I designed a program that would be jointly operated by four patient-led groups with the staff serving as a fifth group. The patient-led groups were to be responsible for their members in carrying out their hospital assignments, taking their prescribed medication, completing group work projects, and the like. The staff served as teachers—giving them feedback about their group functioning and their individual adjustment. This patient-led group ward was to be compared with a typical ward operated in the usual staff-controlled manner.

It seemed that the best procedure was to begin the new program as a pilot program before the research began so that difficulties in the program plan could be identified and changed before the research started. The staff was assembled and told about the new program and the developmental nature of it at this stage. The staff consisted of the supportive psychiatrist, myself, a social worker, a nurse, and two aides.

After they had been assembled, I said, "Now this is a new program for which none of us has been completely trained. Mainly it consists of sharing the responsibility of the patients' recovery with the patients themselves. We'll have to get four rooms on the ward where they can meet privately—without any of us present—to take up and solve the problems of their members. They will meet with us once a week so that we can review their recommendations and we, as a group, will vote on whether to accept all of them; accept some and reject others; or reject them all. One of the most important recommendations is for the group to decide at which level of adjustment each member is now functioning. They will determine the progress each member is making under their supervision and the group and each individual will be rewarded accordingly. I have developed four levels of functioning for each member from level one, which consists of the simple tasks like making one's bed, bathing, etc. through two additional steps of improved responsible behavior accompanied by increasing rewards until the final level of planning the community life for members who have progressed to this level. Groups will be assigned a job for their group to do each day as well as the daily personal chores I just mentioned. Our job will be to suggest alternatives to their judgments when they are unacceptable to us and to encourage them when they are good. As they progress the group and individual members' rewards will be increased, but if they do not progress, there will be no increase in rewards. Our role essentially is to teach, encourage and reward the groups and their members for solving their own problems so that when they leave the hospital they will be able to adjust to community life. Now are there any questions?"

The nurse, Mrs. Tilton, immediately spoke up.

"I'm all for it. I have thought for a long time that these patients should help each other more and should be less reliant upon us."

"Well, that's what it's all about," I answered.

Mrs. Fernandez, an attendant, then stated, "I'm only an attendant, and I don't know anything about this. What am I supposed to do?"

"We'll help you develop a new role," I responded. "As an example, instead of making a member's bed who refuses to do so you will simply tell the group leader that this member did not make his bed and let the group work out a solution in their own meeting. If they do a good job they'll be rewarded—if not, they will not receive a reward. The idea is that working together on problems will be therapeutic in many ways, not the least of which is learning to understand and help each other. After all none of them or any of us, for that matter, lives in a situation where we do not depend on others. In fact, that's the basic definition of a society."

Mrs. Fernandez continued, "I can see that, but what about this business of making judgments about how good their decisions are. Am I expected to do that?"

"Yes," I replied, "you are to participate in making those decisions with other staff members, and here is how we'll do it. We'll meet with each group once a week, and we'll have a list of the problems they have been given. Their secretary will submit in writing to us the solutions their group has made. I'll have copies made, and we'll adjourn to my office where we'll discuss and vote on each one. Each person will have one vote and the majority will decide what is an appropriate decision."

"But," Mrs. Fernandez interjected, "I don't know if my decision will be very good. I've never made any in the hospital, and besides, we have always been told that only the professional staff has enough training and knowledge to make decisions about mental patients."

"Would you mind telling me if you have any children, Mrs. Fernandez?" I asked.

"I have four," she said proudly.

"Don't you make decisions for them and/or help them to make decisions as they get older," I asked.

"Of course," she replied.

I continued, "Then you probably have more knowledge learned in a real-life setting than any of us here. That's the point of this whole approach—it is intended to maximize the contributions of every patient and staff member on this diverse ward."

The meeting ended with the nurse agreeing to work with the attendants in finding space for the patient group meetings and to meet again on the next day.

As soon as the next meeting began the social worker said, "All of you know that a person's departure plans have to be okayed by the department of social work. If these persons are to participate in their own members' community plans, how will that work?"

"I have given a good deal of thought to that problem and others like it," I answered. "What I think would work best is that all of us in our own specialties become consultants to the groups. Suppose the members are planning for a particular member's community adjustment. They would have to submit a plan to you and you could then give them information about how realistic the plan was and recommend changes that might be needed. Where there are specific legal barriers, that would have to be explained to them. Such back and forth exchanges should result in a final plan of departure that you, the rest of the staff, the patient group, and the individual agree upon."

"That sounds reasonable, but I'll have to get it cleared first," he responded.

Later he did, and this established the precedent that if an emergency arose or for any other reason the patient-led group leader could request a consultation with the appropriate staff member.

Finally the time arrived to discuss the proposal with the patients. I called a meeting with them and described in great detail how the system of autonomous group meetings and their participation in them would work.

After the explanation, one patient immediately responded, "We can't make any decisions. The docs won't let us and besides what do we know?"

I answered, "You know a great deal about

mental illness and the problems of adjustment."

"That's right," he replied, "But so what—who cares?"

"We do," I replied. "All I ask is that you give the program of joint participation by the group members and staff a chance."

Another patient then said, "I've tried everything, and so far nothing helps much. This is my tenth year in and out of the hospital. I'd like to try something new. At least I think I know what doesn't work."

And so the process of assigning members to groups began. When it was completed, each group elected its chairman and secretary. With this background, the program began.

As with all new programs, we immediately ran into a problem. When the groups had their meetings, a staff member entered the room with them and told them about the problems they needed to solve for the day. It soon became apparent that the group was turning this period of problem information into a discussion in which they repeatedly wanted to know what the staff member would do. I called a staff meeting and asked the members, "Do the patients ask you what to do in the problem discussion meetings?" Mrs. Tilton, the nurse, answered, "Of course they do. I believe what they really want is for us to tell them what we want them to do. The problem they are solving is 'tell me teacher what's the right answer.' They're responding like my child learning math. She isn't as concerned about learning math as she is about learning what makes her teacher happy. These people have learned over the years to give the staff the answers they want. Somehow we need to let them solve the problems and then we'll give them feedback. That way they'll learn to depend on each other to solve their problems rather than on us."

"That observation is very important," I added, "because it is precisely what we found in our group process studies. They do much better in solving their problems when we are not there. The only technique that I can think of where we wouldn't be present at all but could still give them problems that they need to solve would be one in which we would write out the problems they are to address and get written responses about their solutions from them. Then and only then would we give them feedback about the validity of their judgment. In this way they'd better prepare themselves for community living when we are not there."

"Fine," replied Mrs. Tilton, "we'll begin that tomorrow." Thus we began what later was called "the note system." A box containing problems to be solved by the group was placed near their conference room. These "notes" were picked up each day by the group secretary.

After adopting the "note system" another problem soon emerged. Eddie Smith, the chairman of one of the groups asked to see me. In that meeting he said, "We've got a real problem, doc."

"What is it?" I asked.

He continued, "The staff won't let us solve our own problems. They'll come into our room when we are arguing and tell us to be quiet. Yesterday while we were trying to discuss with Tom why he wouldn't make his bed, the attendant came in and said she had made Tom's bed for him. So what could we do?"

"Well, I'll talk to the staff about these intrusions and try to get them to let your group make their own decisions," I responded.

These intrusions arose over and over again for several months. It was difficult for the staff to adjust to its new role of consultant rather than that of field boss. Finally, after several weeks the new roles became routine just in time for another problem to emerge.

The occupational therapist came up to me in the hall and announced, "We cannot arrange for the groups to do group work. We only have supervised individual work in the hospital and there is no group work."

"Well, let's create some," I responded.

"No," he said, "we'll not be able to help you. I've talked to my boss and he says just tell you there can be no group work."

"I was hoping we could work something out— it's not too difficult," I answered.

"No," he said, "we cannot do it."

So, again I met with Bob Morse and told him of

the problem. He replied, "Well, okay, then we'll do it. You work on some group tasks and let me know and we'll implement them." From this discussion work crews, a patient operated hospital newspaper, and other programs operated by the patient groups were born.

But another problem in the group decision-making soon occurred. It was that groups often made decisions that they failed to carry out. At this early stage of group development, such differences were often easy to find. In the second week of group development, Group A agreed that unless one of its members started making his bed, he could not go with the group on a group picnic. They took him anyway. The staff called this to the group's attention. After several such instances with every group, the groups learned to see to it that their decisions were carried out. This group practice formed a link between verbal behavior (the decision) and action (carrying out the decision). As this change and the others just mentioned occurred leaders emerged in the groups and they slowly began to lead the group in solving their members' problems.

At this time, dramatic changes in both patient and staff morale occurred. Mrs. Tilton stopped me in the hall after the groups had achieved some autonomy.

She began, "This is the most exciting program I have ever been associated with. The staff is so happy they aren't police persons anymore.

Patients don't perceive them as people who force them to do what they should do. All that is handled by their group members. We all dread the day when the experiment will end and we'll have to go back to our usual supervisory roles."

"Maybe you won't," I responded, "maybe the hospital will adopt the program and you can help train other staffs."

"I'd really like that. I hope it happens," she said with a smile.

The patient groups became more and more helpful to their members and the members insisted that their leaders be helpful to the group members. One group secretary asked to see me one day. He seemed very excited and said, "Doc, I'm the new group leader—we had to fire Larry because he didn't take his job seriously. We are tired of his taking drugs and drinking on the weekends so that he sleeps most of the time and doesn't help us anymore. He was so good at the beginning, but he can't handle freedom. We're also going to recommend that he receive no weekend passes for a while."

"That sounds very worthwhile as a recommendation, but as you know, the staff will have to vote on your group's recommendations," I responded.

"That's fine," he answered, "they're usually fair."

Just as the patient groups and the staff had successfully mastered their new roles, a new issue arose. Bob Morse asked me to spend some time with him as soon as possible, so I left my office and went to meet him in his office. When I walked in he began, "You've heard of the 'best laid plans of mice and men . . .' well, guess what just happened. I got a call from Dr. Fischer this morning and he said that he didn't like our program and he thought it might be a malpractice item. I asked him what he meant and he said that the patients should not be making decisions. I told him that all of their decisions were approved by the staff and if they were not approved, the group was asked to change them. He then said that we should treat them as patients and tell them what to do. Besides, he added that they make so much noise talking and arguing that he can hear them even when he walks down the road in front of the building. Anyway I told him that your studies showed a 75% return rate for the long-term mentally ill and that's what we were trying to do something about. I told him I was pleased with the program and that I supported it. As you know, he is a psychoanalyst, and some of them are true believers. He stated we should be doing psychoanalytically-oriented psychotherapy. I told him that with these long-termers, your research showed that individual and group psychotherapy did not seem to help them make a community adjustment."

"So what did he say to that?" I asked.

"'To hell with your goddamn research results,"

he said to me.

Finally, in desperation I said, "I've been analyzed seven different times and it didn't help me. Why should it help them?" I finally told him I would operate my program the way I thought was best for the patients and he should run his program the way that he thought was most helpful."

"Is there anything special that I could do?" I queried.

"Mainly I wanted to tell you before you heard it from someone else. I don't want you to get discouraged from what others say. We know what's happening—the program works, it's that simple," he answered.

And so we avoided another attempt to shut down the program. The groups continued to improve their performance as time went on. As the patient-led groups became more adaptive, their members faced leaving the hospital and the other group members. When this occurred, the four group leaders asked to see me.

The spokesman for the leaders said, "We would like some changes in our procedures. First of all, if we are going to help the members get jobs, they are going to have to take days out of the hospital for job searches. So we'd like to change the rules to permit that."

"That sounds realistic," I answered, "but as always, you'll have to take it up with the staff for their approval."

"Fine," the spokesman continued, "but we

have another problem. The other problem is that the employment offices operated in the hospital and in the community haven't gotten any of our members jobs. We take tests until we're tired and we know from them what our interests and abilities are but the question remains—where are the jobs? So we have decided that we could do better ourselves. We'd like to set up our own job search program and run it our way."

"How would you do that?" I inquired.

"We thought if you could get us a room, the four leaders could interview those who need employment and try to find them jobs. If the agencies can't help us and the counseling service can't help, then we'll have to solve the problem ourselves. In fact we went out last weekend and found two or three places that are interested in interviewing some of our members," he answered.

"Where were they?" I asked.

"On Brand Street. It's only three blocks from here. We found a machine shop that wants sweepers to clean up the shop in the evening. They need at least two and possibly three people and we have three people that are interested. And we can find many more because we have worked out there and we know some other places that may be interested in hiring our members," he added.

"That sounds interesting," I replied, "so take it up with the staff."

"We will," Sam responded.

Within a week they were interviewing the

graduates and their placement record was surprising. They placed every person who wanted a job. Later Mrs. Tilton said to me, "The difference is the motivation. The people who give the tests and do the interviewing have nothing to lose— they simply send the person out to be interviewed. Here the leaders themselves hunt down the jobs and they train the members in interviewing techniques. As we used to say in high school, 'it's a whole different ball game.'"

And there were other surprises involving the caring attitude that had developed among the members. Soon after the employment group was formed, I was walking across the grounds when I saw several members of a group carrying one of their members. I stopped and inquired, "What are you people doing?"

One of the members quickly responded, "We are carrying Eric to lunch. He hurt his legs and can't walk."

I replied, "Why doesn't he eat on the ward?"

"We always have such a good time at lunch that he wanted to come with us so we are taking him," he answered.

"Yeah," responded Eric. How do you like my new Cadillac?"

We all laughed and the group went on to lunch.

But the surprises did not end. On evaluation day with one of the groups, the leader looked at me and stated, "All of us on the ward have decided that we are going to have a picnic for the staff. We have received permission to use the hospital grounds and we want to do all the cooking, clean-up and so on. Would the staff be willing to come?"

Mrs. Tilton replied, "You bet I'll be there, and I want to say thank you, right now." One by one the rest of the staff said they would be pleased to come to the picnic. And so a rollicking evening was had by all.

At the party Bob Morse looked at me and said, "If the general public was here they wouldn't even know who the mentally ill are, and that's as it should be."

"Absolutely," I replied.

The day finally came when the experiment ended and we began to assess its validity. In every adjustmental measure taken in the hospital, the patient's behavior, attitudes and future expectancies were highly significantly more adaptive compared with the ward under the traditional program. But alas, these well-behaved and happy persons—even when most had employment upon leaving—returned to the hospital at rates similar to those in the earlier studies. Seventy-five percent of the long-term mentally ill returned within eighteen months. As they came back to the hospital, they were interviewed. And one person summarized the reaction of all of the returnees in their common response. When I asked him, "Why did you return—you did so well in the hospital, you were a group leader, everyone on the ward, patients and staff alike, thought you did so well. What happened?"

He replied, "Here I was accepted as an important member of the group—someone others could rely on—someone you and the staff as well as the group members could look up to. When I got out there I was a mentally ill person who others were afraid of and disliked. I have thought about it a lot and I have talked to others about it and we all missed the support and help of our group members. When we were here, the other members would see us through these types of reactions by the public. I didn't have that support and the load got too heavy to carry so I returned here for help— mostly for acceptance and support."

It was this sort of common response that led me to discuss the results further with Bob Morse. I mentioned to him, "With this sort of evidence, we ought to move these groups into the community and see if they can support each other there."

"I have reached the same conclusion, but we must incorporate the central fact that we learned here—they will only succeed if they can operate their own programs. They have to be involved and they have to actually operate the program themselves. Of course, you'll have to train them to do so," he responded.

"That is exactly what I have concluded. That's what I intend to do," I answered. And so the community venture began.

CHAPTER 5
Moving into Community Reality

What became apparent from all of our scientific information was that these people needed to establish an entirely new role and social position for themselves. This was the result of ten years' research experience and reminded me of my statistics teacher's comment many years ago: "It's only through successive experiments aimed at problem solution that an answer to a research question will emerge."

Since we now knew the needed roles were not available in the society at the present time it seemed necessary to create a small society within the larger society so that these people's needs could be met. What came to mind again was the small groups that the immigrants had established in the early years of our country. They formed small societies where the cultural procedures with which they were familiar could be practiced. They protected and helped one another. To a certain extent their language formed a barrier between those who spoke the same language and others who did not. Yet their own small society protected and helped them eventually make an adjustment to the broader society. Such adjustmental patterns were inherent in the formation of the American society even though the assimilation process took many years for some and was never fully completed for others.

This general pattern seemed to have relevance here because these individuals needed to have some sort of social support system that was not totally contingent upon the larger society to maintain. This seemed an especially important social model since our research clearly showed that these mentally ill persons could solve problems in groups; almost all had no place to live since they had "worn out" their welcome with family and friends; they needed a place to be employed if they were to support themselves; they needed medical attention; they needed social relations with others; and above all they needed protection from a hostile environment. Furthermore, it also seemed clear that these needs would exist for these particular persons for a long period of time—probably years. My conclusion was that an entirely new small-scale society would have to be created and maintained in the community with new roles for the mentally ill and the professionals alike. The first task to establish this small society was to try to create a small problem-solving group that was interested in participating in such an adventure.

I thought that this was likely because of the continuing return to the mental hospital of so many of them. Indeed, a number of such persons had never left the hospital since entering it which in some cases was many years. So one day I began asking the patients if they would be interested in attempting to start such a society provided I could come up with the money and housing to start this enterprise. To my surprise one out of every two persons I talked to not only was interested but asked me to begin the program as soon as possible. With this encouragement I decided to move ahead.

But, of course, this would also have to be established as an experiment since we needed to know what its processes and outcomes would be. The success of the small group program in the hospital and the failure of its members to remain in the community provided the logical background for starting this project as a research. The final research would compare this new small group program located in the community with the existing community mental health programs.

Twenty-five male patients became the first volunteer members of the society. Later there would be many more. They were indeed a diverse group of men varying in age from 21 to 60; most with psychotic diagnoses; some talked a lot and some hardly talked at all; some were quite rational while others made little sense; some had strange mannerisms and some did not. But most important they all expressed a desire to enter the community and become participating citizens—a wish that might be very hard to fulfill. Nonetheless, we had begun an enterprise that would affect all of our lives.

It seemed important from the outset that the group should be trained to rely upon me as little as possible since total independence and citizenship responsibilities of all the members was the goal once they were in the community. Accordingly, I called the first meeting and asked them to elect a chairman and secretary. I left the meeting so they could have their privacy to make the selections. They were also told to send the chairman to my office after the election and to record the vote so that I would know who was elected and by what type of majority. At this point, I left the meeting room and returned to my office.

About two hours later, I heard a knock on the door and left my desk to open it. In front of me stood a rather small, thin man who announced, "I am Jack Edwards and I am the newly elected leader of the group."

"Hello, Mr. Edwards," I replied, but before I asked him if he had the ballots he reached into his pocket and handed me 25 small sheets of paper. Then he looked at me and said, "My name appeared on twenty-four of the ballots along with the name of Eddie Watson, who was later unanimously elected to be the secretary of the group. It looks like we'll be doing a lot of business together."

I replied, "We certainly will, and I would like you to understand that the move into the community will take a great deal of effort. We will have to work closely together. In this regard, I'll communicate with you and you can tell the group—of course. I've already told all the members in our initial get-acquainted meeting that they can see me at any time. I would like to see you and the newly elected secretary at ten o'clock tomorrow."

Promptly at ten the next morning, I heard a knock at the office door and there were the two group members.

"Doc," Jack said, "this is Eddie Watson, the new secretary, and he would like to be called Eddie. I saw several members last night and we all agreed that we'd call you Doc, and we would like for you to learn all of our first names and call us by them. That's important to us because if we are going to have our own business, and so forth, we would like to act as partners."

"That's fine with me," I declared. "Well, come on in and have a seat and we'll get down to business. The first thing we need to begin is the plan for moving into the community. In order to accomplish a plan that is essentially yours, I am going to give you a problem about community living for the group to solve every day. You will hold your own private meetings, but at the end of each day you, Eddie, will need to give me a written plan that has been agreed upon by the group. I'll read it carefully and give you a written response about the validity of your plan in that area by eight o'clock the next morning. If the plan is unacceptable, I will tell you why in my written response and, Jack, you can call another meeting and revise the plan until we both agree that the plan sounds feasible. Over a period of time, we will resolve all the areas of planning we need to complete in order to move into the community. Do you understand what I am proposing?"

Jack spoke up immediately and said, "I believe I understand it okay, but why all the meetings and all the writing?"

"Well," I answered, "my own experience and the research information shows that when patients meet with staff they're so willing to please the staff person that they often say things they believe the staff person would like to hear. Our purpose here is different. There are 25 brains in the group and if all 25 members are allowed to make a plan for the entire group it is likely to be a much better plan than one person would make. Besides I want it to be mainly your plan so that the group members will support it. After all, if you make your own plan, it should represent the best judgment of the group. This is particularly true if no plan can be activated that is not approved by two-thirds of the group and approved by me. So let's get started. Here's some paper and pencils. You'll notice on the top sheet I have placed the problem for today. It is 'What kind of housing shall we get for this group of twenty-five men?'"

Jack and Eddie stared at me and Jack quietly said, "We'll try but you'll have to be patient because we've never done anything like this before."

And Eddie added, "I don't think I've ever been asked to plan my future. Mostly the docs want to know about my earlier life, my brother and sisters, my parents and things like that. I hope I haven't been in here too long so that I can have a future. Mostly it's do what you're told and don't worry about the future. I really hope the group members can do this."

"I wouldn't have asked you to make such plans if I didn't think this group could make a meaningful plan. At any rate go and try," I replied.

The group made a decision on a new area of their community life every day. The final plan included a cafe business with an accountant, supervisors and workers, cooks and housekeepers, and a recreational director.

The next issue was how to implement the plan. Obviously they would need money for housing, business start-up and the like. And so the money chasing act began. Telephone calls placed to the usual program development groups in mental illness indicated that they were not interested in any program designed to create gradually a small society and turn it over to the group members regardless of what they did in adjustmental terms. A common response was, "What are you trying to do, Bill, give our jobs away?" Another less common statement, but implying the same negative reaction was, "We have worked very hard to create this system, and now you are trying to destroy it." It seemed clear to me that my naivete was due to a difference in my perception of what treating mental illness was all about. I had always thought that treatment programs were designed for the mentally ill, not for the service providers. To check on my perceptions, I called my psychiatrist friend, Bob Morse, and told him of the reaction of many of our colleagues.

"Well," he mused, "I wonder if those people ever thought that without these sick people they would be without a job!" He continued, "It shows clearly that you're going to have to go outside the fraternity if you want to get funds for this project. I suppose what it really shows is that money and power—and in our society money is power—are the basic ingredients. When money and power needs are satisfied—and they may never be for some people—then we can turn our attention to humanitarian concerns!"

"Well, Bob, I appreciate your remarks and I'll now turn my attention to other possible sources of support," I replied. But I had also begun to learn that the establishment priorities were upside down—at least from my perspective.

So the search began. I had known a social

worker, Claire Keller, for some time. I had discussed this potential project with her and she became quite interested in it, in fact, she had told me that if I needed any help to look her up and she'd try to help me in any way she could. So without any further hesitation I called her and told her of the financing problem. "Maybe I can help," she responded. "Give me a week and then we'll get together and see what we can come up with."

"Fine, I'll meet you in my office Monday morning at nine," I said. She arrived at my office on Monday morning precisely at nine. She told me she had some good news. She said she was associated with a church group that represented the entire state and that she had presented this idea to their finance committee. One member owned an old motel which was very liveable, but since the new freeway had been built it was rarely ever completely occupied. In view of this situation, he offered to work with the group so that they could use the motel as a residence.

Claire remarked, "I told him he'd have to take a risk that they would eventually make enough money to lease the property, but this could only come after the group had built a business and had become financially secure. I also mentioned to him that they could pay a little rent from the outset since some received disability income from various sources."

"This sounds good to me," I told Claire, "and I

will bring this information to the group as soon as possible."

Since it appeared that we could get housing, it seemed to me that the next important step was to look into how a business could be started. I called my lawyer friend who was in corporate law and told him of the plan. He, too, showed a strong interest and offered to be the group's lawyer in an attempt to help them form their own corporation.

He further declared, "Whether the corporation would be profit or nonprofit would be up to the group to decide, but the clear advantage is that a business organized in this fashion can set its own employment rules for its members."

"This sounds good to me," I responded.

It seemed particularly good to me since I knew that with the members' disabilities there would undoubtedly be times when a member could not carry out his work assignment. As an employee in a traditional company, he would probably be fired and lose any source of income to say nothing of his self-confidence. But a corporation owned by the members could establish its own work attendance plans. A corporation also had the advantage that the members could establish their own pay rates, employment training, management, and so on, which might be quite different than the usual corporate procedures.

The lawyer then said, "When the appropriate time comes, I will meet with the group and discuss with them how to set up a corporation and all of the legal procedures involved."

As I left his office, I began to feel at least some confidence that the program could be activated.

But a proper health program raised another critical issue. For advice and discussion of this matter, I again sought out my psychiatrist friend, Bob Morse. We had a long discussion about the health needs of the group, particularly in view of the group members' willingness to become productive citizens after such a long time in the mental hospital. He offered this opinion: "The physician that the people need will be someone who shares their philosophical position and one who will not interfere with the society's activities. It should be someone that the members can see when they want to like any person in the community."

This information now needed to be given to the group for their comments about whether or not they agreed with the medical part of the plan. I therefore asked to see Jack, the chairman, upon my return to the office. He soon appeared and I presented the plan to him. He listened carefully and said, "It sounds okay to me, but I'll have to check with the members." He then called a meeting of the group.

Soon after their meeting, the members agreed to see a community physician for their medication and other medical needs. The group decided that the members should accept the motel offer and start visiting the motel which the owner would lease to them. Their plan was to assign rooms to the members, make certain the rooms were clean, learn about the kitchen, make the beds and examine equipment required for daily living. In this way, they attempted to prepare themselves for the move from the hospital to the community. So the daily visiting began and after two weeks, the group met and decided that it was time to go to their new home. Prior to the move, however, I had some negotiating to do with the hospital staff. They agreed that should anyone in the group need hospital care, they would be immediately admitted to the hospital. But along with this agreement was one of extreme importance for this fledgling group. It was that every patient was discharged from the mental health system upon leaving the hospital for their new abode. This was an important step since I had continually insisted that they were responsible citizens and that they would need to take care of themselves and each other upon leaving the hospital. It, of course, was also made clear to them that I had found a physician that they could see in the community like any other citizen. This move was made in an attempt to allay their fears about the all-encompassing mental health system that wouldn't let them go and at the same time would not grant them full citizenship. It was my hope that they would now see that our words matched our deeds, that we meant what we said about their responsibility as citizens. The crux of the plan, therefore, was to provide a safety net for them should they fail individually or as a group but to let them know that we expected them to succeed.

On a Monday morning, we embarked on the journey that none of us, at that time, could clearly appreciate. A bus took the members to the leased motel and I followed an hour or so later in my car. Imagine my surprise when I arrived at the motel and no one was there. I knew the bus had been there because suitcases were everywhere, but no people. I went into the motel and sat down to try to collect my thoughts. What had happened? Hadn't they agreed to meet with me when I arrived so that we could discuss further the first week's plan? After about two hours, the members started to drift in. First, came their leader, Jack, and the secretary, Eddie.

Jack was smiling and swaggering in his walk as he announced, "Doc, forget the plan to open a restaurant, I just made a deal to buy some property and build an amusement park. We'll run the park for the kids in the neighborhood. That way we'll all have work and a business of our own."

"There's one serious problem with that plan," I mused, "it is that the group has very little money. How do you plan to buy the land?"

"Well, we thought that you would loan us the money to buy it," he replied.

"Unfortunately, I don't have that kind of money," I retorted, "but if I did, I don't think I'd invest it in that plan. I think you had better go talk to whomever you made the deal with, and tell them that it won't work."

"Well, okay, but I'm really crushed, Doc. I thought you had plenty of money, and that you'd think this was a great idea." he murmured.

"You're wrong on both counts," I countered.

Soon the others drifted into the motel. As they came in, I asked each one where he had been. Some said, "to a local bar"; others said they had "gone to a show"; one had gone "to pet a horse in a neighbor's yard"; and so on. As I talked to each one, what suddenly occurred to me was that these people were acting like other people who get released from long-term confinement. They were behaving like the warden in the prison said prisoner's behaved when released. Their primary attitude was that, "I'm now a citizen. I can do what I please." Apparently, the freedom of citizenship had been clearly understood by them, but not the responsibilities. It seemed obvious to me that the responsibility side of the citizenship equation would need a great deal of work. This became clearer an hour or so later when several of the members entered the restaurant and demanded their dinner. I mentioned to them that they had planned the first meal in the hospital and had selected a cook. John, the elected cook then spoke up, "I would get supper, but I can't cook."

"Why in the hell did you agree to be cook in our meeting then?" Jack asked.

"I couldn't do anything else so I thought

maybe I could learn to cook," answered John.

"Well, Doc, what are we going to eat?" said another member, Frank.

"You have a checking account and it's only five blocks to the store. That's as much as I can do for you. I'm going home now to be with my family, and I'll be back to check everything out around nine tonight." As I drove away, I wondered what they would do. But I did know that they could solve the eating problem if they decided that they wanted to.

When I arrived home, my wife, Betty, said, "How did it go?"

I replied, "We've just entered the reality phase in community living."

That evening I returned to the motel. The smell of cooked food was in the air as I walked into the restaurant. Several members were finishing their meals and two others were washing and drying dishes.

Jack approached me and said, "We worked it out. We found out that Wishner could really cook, and so we got a week's supply of groceries and fixed the meal. Everyone pitched in so it worked out okay as long as we all worked together."

Doc he continued, "We all appreciate what you are trying to do for us and we'll do our best to make things work out. We all agreed on one thing while you were gone and it is that you are either the most courageous person we've ever met or you're crazier than hell. Who else would come out into the community like this with a bunch of nuts."

I replied, "Well, Jack, only time will tell."

The next morning, when I arrived at the motel, I found everyone fed, clothed and sitting around. I called a meeting and asked the group, "When are you going to start the restaurant business that you have spent so much time planning to do in the hospital?"

One of the members, Smitty, remarked, "I really don't think we should start a restaurant. I think the restaurant section of the motel is too small to accommodate us and the public. I think we ought to rethink the business that we want to start." I noticed that almost every person there began nodding his head.

"Fine," I asserted, "let's begin a new plan." There was no dearth of plans mentioned from a motorcycle repair shop to a construction company. But then I inquired, "What skills do you have that would permit you to operate a business?" Lengthy discussions followed with several persons giving a detailed account of their work histories.

Finally, Eddie spoke up, "We all have done so many different things that it's going to have to be something all of us can do. What I've been thinking is that we could operate a janitorial service." While Eddie was speaking, Harry and Pete were hallucinating and Ira was sitting there with the anvil he had made which he always carried with him.

Eddie continued, "If we do settle on a janitorial

company, that means that Pete and Harry will have to stop talking to themselves all the time and Ira you'll have to leave your anvil at home. It's a shame both of you will have to do this but you know how the people are out there. You see," Eddie went on, "they're all crazy."

"Can you clarify that for me?" I inquired.

"Doc," Eddie responded, "You of all people should know that carrying a small, handmade anvil around and talking to someone out loud who is not there is okay. There is nothing wrong with that as far as I'm concerned. But the public can't stand it. It's okay with us here if they do it in our house, the public doesn't see them and if it doesn't interfere with their work, I wouldn't care if they did it on the job. But you see the people out there believe there is something wrong with anyone who would do those things, and so if we want to stay out here we'll have to watch ourselves when we go into the community. Besides the business, I think we should decide what scares the people out there and behave in such a way that we won't scare them—so that when we go out in the community we appear like everyone else—wear a suit and tie and they'll think we're bankers—because above all none of us here want to go back to the hospital."

"I agree with the janitorial idea," interjected Smitty, "and we should vote on that in a minute, but first I think we ought to adopt a few rules about what is okay in our house and what is okay in public. First, I think we should agree that none of us will go back to the hospital. If someone goes a little crazy for a while we should try to help him over that time until he is okay again because we all have been there and we know that no one wants to go back. So I'd like to ask Jack to take a vote about our first mission that ranks above all else—no return to the hospital. And we'll all be responsible for each other so that no one has to go back."

Jack replied, "I couldn't agree with you more. Let's take a vote on not going back to the hospital as our primary mission." The vote was unanimous. Then Jack said, "Let's also change the restaurant business to a janitorial business. This is a rich area so I'm sure they need lots of people to clean houses. Maybe eventually we'll be able to do maintenance work on some big buildings." Again the vote was unanimous. "Doc, don't you think we ought to talk with that legal guy about a corporation?"

"Yes," I answered, "I'll talk to him this evening."

I went home for that evening feeling we had made some progress. I called the corporate lawyer and he agreed to meet with the group the next day at ten o'clock. I arrived early the next morning to find Jack quite upset.

"What's wrong?" I asked.

Jack responded, "Doc, last night several of us noticed that John was acting strangely. He was talking to himself and seemed angry with everyone. Finally Smitty called several of us aside and said he had counted John's pills and he hadn't taken any for several days. So we told him to get back on his medication like the doctor ordered. He did and he seems okay today, but we called a meeting and agreed that Smitty—who rooms with him—would make sure that he took his medication on time every day until we were certain he could and would continue. So the group voted that Smitty would give him his pills for thirty days. After that we'll see if he can try it alone again. But most important Smitty said he would be our group's nurse to count anyone's pills who begins to act crazy. We think that this way we can live up to our primary goal— don't go back to the hospital."

"Hmmmm." I mused. "Hmmmm."

At ten o'clock the lawyer arrived and the meeting was started. He explained to them in great detail the advantages and disadvantages of profit and nonprofit corporations. The results of this meeting were that the members decided to start a profit making corporation. The corporation was to involve all businesses that the group decided to create. Their first business was to become the janitorial business that they had earlier discussed. The problem now facing the group was, "How do we go about starting a janitorial business?" But for the members this did not pose any difficulty. In their subsequent meeting about the janitorial business, the members took the position that they already knew about janitorial work and therefore all they had to do was announce their business to the public and go to work. There appeared no argument that would persuade them that the janitorial business was a business like any other and that establishing it would require considerable thought and action. So it occurred to me that they should learn by doing and I mentioned their new business to several of my professional friends.

Dr. Johnson, a friend, immediately declared, "I need a great deal of work done at my house and I'd be happy to hire them." When the members got this feedback, they held another meeting and decided that they would work in crews of three members each—a crew chief who was responsible for the entire job, an assistant crew chief who would work with the chief and take responsibility for certain agreed upon areas of work, and a worker who would do whatever job the crew chief or assistant assigned to him.

I was the only one with a car—a station wagon—so Jack and I got into the car to give Dr. Johnson and his family a job estimate. Dr. Johnson had requested an estimate before hiring the group. When we arrived at his house, he met us at the door and showed us the rugs he wanted cleaned and also two rooms that he wanted painted. Then he turned to Jack and said, "What is your estimate?"

Jack looked very thoughtful and finally stated,

"Well, I think we can let you have it for about 10 thou."

"What did you say?" Dr. Johnson asked.

Jack repeated, with some indignity, "Ten thousand."

I entered the discussion and said that Jack and I needed a few minutes to discuss the work and the price. As Dr. Johnson left the room, Jack turned to me and angrily blurted out, "What the hell's wrong with you, I had him going for ten thousand."

"No, you did not," I declared, "—we are going to ask $300.00 dollars."

When Dr. Johnson returned to the room, Jack softly remarked, "We'll sacrifice and do the work for $300.00, but this is only because we are just getting started." All the way back to the motel Jack pouted and kept repeating that I had deprived the group of "ten thou." Upon arrival at the motel, I immediately summoned the group and told them of the event at Dr. Johnson's house. The members adjourned to their meeting and later told me that they were happy with the job and price but that Jack was not to make any more job bids.

Early the next morning a crew of three left with me to go to the Johnson job. My old station wagon had brooms and equipment sticking out the window and the top and I thought this must be interesting to others on the freeway. I dropped the group off at the job and told them I'd return in an hour or two to see how they were doing.

In about two hours, I returned to the first janitorial job. The crew chief greeted me with "Hi ya, Doc" when I entered the house. As I glanced around at their work I couldn't believe my eyes. This must have been one of the poorest and strangest performances by a janitorial crew anywhere. The painting was, to speak bluntly, horrible. The trim around the baseboard was in a different shade, if not a different color. Painting of the baseboards was extended to the wall itself in many places. Floors were dirty but everyone was smiling.

"What do you think, Doc," one of the workers asked.

"Well," I said "this is not done correctly so we'll have to start over and this time I'll supervise the work. And so, we spent the rest of the day retouching and reworking the job until it was completed as a good service would do. But more important, it had become very obvious to me that these people did not know how to work—all of their janitorial work in the hospital had not prepared them for this type of competitive work.

When we arrived back at the motel I told Jack what had happened and recommended that they have a meeting to discuss the future of their corporation. Then I went to my office and was met there by two friends—a psychologist and a psychiatrist. When I told them what had happened, I was startled by their response. The psychologist remarked, "Do you mean to tell me that you received your doctorate in order to work as a janitor with these people?" I didn't respond. The division of our society into the "haves" and "have nots" was all too clear in their reaction. It was made even clearer before I left. The psychiatrist stated, "You should make them come to your office for psychotherapy. Then they'll know who is the doctor." What kept running through my mind was that these professionals had no idea what type of subordinate social role the patients had to play. The system demanded it. It made no difference that these people had no jobs, few skills, and most had no interested relatives and were alone. So their therapy would at the very least have to include some way in which they could exist in the community. My professional friends should have paid attention to Maslow who had earlier stated that until basic human needs were fulfilled no amount of free expression has much meaning to low status individuals. Thinking of Maslow's writings and other scholars made me feel better about the route we had chosen. I also thought of a story about Einstein who throughout his life pondered about men's desire to dominate others. "To what end?" he puzzled. Having been poor myself and socially ignored in the past from time to time made me appreciate more than I would ever have thought possible the social position of these social outsiders who our society had all but discarded.

The next morning I returned to the motel and my spirits were lifted dramatically by what I saw and was told. There had been a long meeting which everyone attended during which the members' community life to date was reviewed. During the meeting, several rather far-reaching decisions were made which were to have a continuing impact on the further development of this small democratic society. Generally, they were concerned that they needed to establish some rules and guidelines about their work and their living situation. Jack handed me a list of house rules that they had unanimously agreed should be adopted. These mainly consisted of issues about personal cleanliness, getting to meals on time, no drinking alcohol for those who had a demonstrated drinking problem, taking medication on time and so on. And equally important, they adopted a number of work rules. No one could live there who would not help with the work, but the work would be pitched at a level that each person could accomplish. They would hire a janitorial consultant and this consultant would help them establish a training program that all members would have to pass before going to work on a paying job. A pay scale would be established with each person's pay determined by the responsibility of the role and its technical nature.

Soon after I was informed of all these decisions, the janitorial consultant arrived. After introductions, he began discussing with them the nature of the business and how to develop it. It seemed clear to me that I should leave and let them work on their business organization. As I was preparing to leave, Jack walked out of the building with me.

"I think everything is going to be okay," he murmured. And then he glanced out at the freeway where an accident had occurred and the traffic was piled up for miles. He looked at the long lines of stalled traffic and shook his head. Suddenly he turned to me and said with a smile, "And to think that those people sitting there in this heat think we're crazy."

When I arrived at my home I received a telephone call from one of the member's mothers. She immediately informed me that she had heard from her son that the group was starting a janitorial corporation and she was very disturbed by such an action. "After all," she elaborated, "Harry went to college and I would rather he not work at all than to work as a janitor." I tried to explain to her that one of the advantages of owning a business was that a member could move up and down the organizational ladder from worker to manager without moving out of the organization. Nevertheless, she insisted that her son was not going to work as a janitor.

At that point, I remarked, "If I remember correctly, Harry has not worked for five years and has never held a full-time job. Maybe this is an opportunity for him to start a work career."

The next day I returned to the motel and Harry met me as I drove in and stated, "Please don't pay any attention to my mother. She called me last night after talking to you and told me to get out of here and return to the hospital. She said janitorial work was not good for me. So I asked her if I could come home and she said, 'Absolutely not! You're sick and you should be in the hospital.' When I told her I thought I was doing fine here she said how embarrassed she was that I was nothing but a janitor. It's always been the same with her—she has always liked me when I did precisely what she wanted. So I told her I was not going back to the hospital unless I had to and that all of us in the group had set staying out of the hospital and earning our own way in the community as best we could as goals. But she found trouble with that, too. 'You've been brainwashed,' she said, 'That group is bad for you. They even seem to think they can run a business. What a laugh.' And I said, 'I've got news for you. I am happy here and I'm doing well for the first time in a long time. I am going to stay. After all, we can go whenever we want and we all have a voice in this program. I know you would have liked me to be a doctor or lawyer, but I couldn't, so now I'm going to try to do as good as I can. These people are my friends. They want me to succeed.'"

I couldn't escape seeing the similarity between how some of my colleagues felt about my interest in starting this program and Harry's mother's perception. Both Harry's mother and my colleagues didn't think we should be involved in janitorial work. The social definition of various jobs in our society could not have been more clearly expressed. I thought, *it's amazing that people so readily divide their environment into 'do's' and 'don'ts,' especially when janitorial work itself has no inherent good or bad in it. Maybe this tells us something about ourselves and our society.*

I then told Harry to do whatever he thought was best for him and I left to see what had been established for the training procedures. What a surprise! Eddie and Joe were busy writing instruction manuals and as I came by, Eddie glanced up and remarked, "The consultant told us we should have a training manual, so we were trying to write one. He also told us that we should write one for each job-crew chief, assistant chief, and worker. So we're trying. Would you read it when we're done and see if it reads okay?"

"Sure," I responded, "I'd be happy to," and indeed I would. I then went into the office and Alex, who had become bookkeeper, said he was trying to understand bookkeeping and its techniques.

He elaborated, "You know, Doc, I took bookkeeping in high school but I haven't looked at a set of books since then, but I'm trying, and I think I'll be able to learn how to do it."

He then turned to me and with a great deal of intensity said, "You know, Doc, I often thought that I was discriminated against because my skin color is black, and I'm sure sometimes I was. But, man, that's nothing compared to what it's been since I was diagnosed as a schizophrenic at the hospital. When I go home, no one will talk to me. When I go into the restaurant or bar, they all leave. Everyone near my home knows that I'm a schizo and they want nothing to do with me. They act like they're going to become mentally ill by being near me. When I try to tell them I don't feel any different than I used to, they just walk away. Boy, I'm telling you this schizophrenia is something else. They seem to think that all schizophrenics are bad. That we will hurt them. Parents take their kids away when they see me coming. Even my own family doesn't want me around."

"Yes," I confided, "that's the trouble with labels. They soon become symbols for something often unintended by their creators. But they can make life miserable for a person nonetheless. Remember one thing—you're just as good as anyone no matter what your diagnosis. You have learned what schizophrenia is in the hospital and you also have learned that it, in itself, is merely a medical diagnosis. So simply be the good person we both know you are and don't worry about psychiatric terminology."

As we parted, I thought of the paradox in trying to diagnose the mentally ill—we often give them labels that discourage others from interacting with them—life is difficult enough for them without any added burden. This sparked a memory of the story a young psychiatrist from Vietnam had told me.

His story made much more sense to me now than it had when I heard it. He told me that prior to the occupation of Vietnam by the French, there had been in the Vietnamese society no diagnosed mental illness. People who behaved differently were given specific roles in society that they could fulfill and they still remained an integral part of the society. There was a Shaman in each village who met the religious and spiritual needs of the village members. In those days, Vietnam was an accumulation of small villages. But once the French arrived, they created the city of Saigon which grew and grew until it was a large metropolis. When this occurred, many people left their villages and moved to the city in an attempt to obtain employment since the center for jobs had been shifted to Saigon. As a young man, he was sent to France to study medicine and he became a psychiatrist. Returning to Vietnam where the French were now in control, he was assigned to a large mental hospital built by the French for the mentally ill. As he began talking to those who were admitted to the hospital, he found that many of them were those who had gotten along well in the villages and some were Shaman whose role in the villages had been to "pray" for people who found these shaman on the street playing their three-string instruments. Since this was their only role, and a much respected one in the villages, they continued their practice in Saigon. Soon they were picked up by the police and eventually they arrived at the mental hospital. The young psychiatrist said that the unfortunate part of the importation of the French and the Western world's culture was that it defined peoples' roles in Western cultural terms thereby creating the mentally ill and mental hospitals. And most important, their approach was to isolate these people from what the French considered the "contributing" members of society. With this thought in mind, I left the motel to return home for a few hours of relaxation.

But my evening of relaxation never occurred. As I reached the front door of my home, Betty yelled, "Someone has been trying to reach you on the phone. Call this number," she said as she handed me a piece of paper with the number on it. The phone rang and John, an assistant crew chief, answered the phone. "Hurry over to 241 Oak Street—we need you."

"I'll be right there," I replied. Arriving at the address, I rang the doorbell and John opened the door. John, escorted me into a large combined kitchen and recreation room. As I glanced about I saw Joe—another crew member standing in the corner mumbling. About the same time, I saw their problem. Frank, the crew chief was being drug around the floor by a floor polishing buffer and appeared to be drunk. Suddenly, Joe burst into laughter and blurted out, "Boy, with a couple of bottles of wine, that Frank can really go."

"Shut off the machine," I yelled to Frank.

He did and almost fell to the floor. Joe and I grabbed him while Frank mumbled that he was okay and needed to finish the job. With that all three of us helped Frank into my car.

"I've never seen anything like that," Joe said. Suddenly we all laughed as Joe added, "You'd pay a hell of a price to see that at a movie. His dancing around behind that buffer was—well, something else."

"Where did he get the wine?" I asked.

"In the cupboard," Joe responded.

"You two finish the job and I'll take Frank home. I'll come back soon and bring some wine replacements with me."

When I arrived at the motel, I met Jack, the manager. Frank mumbled a few words to him and Jack turned to me and said, "You know, Frank has a drinking problem but he hasn't been drinking since we've been here. I'll take him to his room." He did and when he returned he continued, "I know this will be a disappointment to everyone, but actually Frank told me this is the longest period of time he has been without a drink for several years. We'll take this up at a group meeting tonight and decide what to do. I'll check on him every fifteen minutes or so and take him to Doctor Cutler if he has any trouble."

I left to pick up the two replacement bottles of

wine. When I arrived at the house, the job was finished and the house looked freshly scrubbed. As they loaded their equipment into the car, John and Joe burst into laughter and Joe remarked, "I can't wait to see Frank. I think I'll tell him that he won the olympic buffer decathlon."

After leaving them at the motel, I thought about the healing wonders of the comic's statement. "Laugh at yourself and the world laughs with you."

When I arrived at the motel the next morning, I saw Jack, the manager, and he explained, "We met last night and demoted Frank to assistant crew chief. We also docked him a week's pay. We told him if there was a next time, he'd have to leave. We told him our business is more important than any one person. He claims he's off the booze for good. Maybe yes—maybe no—we'll see. But we did send him out to work today with Jim Beck. As you know, he's our best no-nonsense chief. Frank won't pull anything with him or if he does he'll wish he hadn't. We hope it will work."

As I got in my car to leave, I thought—*a penalty—but with a heart*.

But the members of this new small society soon again discovered that they had to establish and live by their own rules if they were to survive. This was clearly illustrated when I arrived at the motel several days later and the members were in a meeting. I sat down and poured myself a cup of coffee and waited until the meeting was over. Jack soon appeared and pronounced, "We've been having a Hell of a time."

"What about?" I inquired.

"Oh, its that damn Fred and Eddie," he blurted out. They came home last night about midnight with two girls. They were all drunk and yelling like hell and that went on for most of the night. Just when I thought I could go to sleep, they started up again. Early this morning the girls came out of their room and they all started yelling again and I went out and told the girls to go home and they said, 'To hell with you.' Well, I said 'You get out of here or I'll call the cops.' They called me every name you can think of and then they left. So I called a meeting right then and there and we've been in conference ever since until right now."

"What happened in the conference?" I queried.

"We argued and argued — called each other names and all that stuff — but finally everyone agreed that we should not bring girls here. Each member can do what he wants — rent a motel, go to the girls house or whatever but, but you cannot bring them here."

"Why did you decide that?" I asked.

"Well, we're trying to establish a good reputation here. In the past there have been prostitutes and drug dealers living here and the neighbors hated them. If we were to have wild parties all the time the neighbors would soon see that we were evicted. And besides we all have to work in the morning. If partying people keep us up all night how can we work the next day? Everyone voted for it except Fred and Eddie and we told them if they didn't like it—move out. They grumbled a while but they're going to stay. Anyway its another rule we'll all have to live by."

"It sounds like it," I replied. "It's a tough rule, since the majority rules I hope you can live by it," I answered.

"Oh we will, we will," Jack said.

In parting I explained, "You're learning what every society had to learn in order to survive. You have to have rules and you have to live by them."

CHAPTER 6
Flight into Business

Despite their emotional and behavioral ups and downs, it now appeared that the governance and business of the small society were developing. Much like planting a seed it would take some time to become a mature plant, but it seemed to me they finally had the right ingredients. As I entered the motel, I realized how far they had come. There was the dining area with its tables clean and shiny. To the right of the dining area was the business office with its manager-book-keeper and his desk, calculator, chair and work pad. A bulletin board was in the entry way with the list of jobs to be done that day with the tools, cleaners, etc. that were required along with the assignment of crews. It did indeed appear to be what they hoped it would be—a thriving business. Even so, most of the jobs came from relatives, acquaintances, and mental health workers who were attempting to help in this neophyte adventure. "Hi, Doc," a voice said. I turned around to see the manager, Jack, entering the room.

"What's new?" I asked.

"We had a meeting last night and we believe we have enough business to buy a new truck. What do you think?" Jack responded.

"How would you pay for it?" I inquired.

"We have enough money for a down payment and our income is certainly high enough to make the monthly payments." Jack elaborated.

"Why don't you call the auditor of the books and see what he says?" I suggested.

"I already asked him and he believes we should get a van as soon as possible. That old station wagon just doesn't do it—no offense, Doc," Jack answered.

"How did he tell you to go about the purchase?" I queried.

"He said he'd call an auto agency that handles the truck we want and he will vouch for our ability to pay for the van," Jack rejoined.

"Well, then go ahead and start planning for the van," I responded.

The next day I returned to the motel to find everyone engaged in training. The janitorial consultant was there and told me how happy he was with the response of the members. About that time the truck driver came over where the janitorial consultant and I were standing and informed me that he was going in to get a cup of coffee. "I love this place," he said. "In fact, it's my favorite place to go on this route."

"Why do you like it so much?" I inquired.

"Because everyone here is so friendly, unlike other places I go. The people will do anything for you. They're just like the people I've been around all my life," he answered.

"Do you find any of them strange?" I asked.

"No, well some of them talk to themselves a bit, and others are sometimes silent when you ask them something, and then there is the guy who carries that anvil around all the time . . . but hey, you should see some of my relatives. They do the same things. These fellows tell me they come from the mental hospital—well, if that's the case, half of my relatives ought to be there. But let me tell you something . . . the other people on my route have never been in the hospital as far as I know, and believe me, these people are much nicer to be around than they are . . . doesn't that tell you something?" he remarked.

"Yes, it does," I replied, and I thought — *far more than you know.*

It was time again to load up the station wagon and head for another customer from the mental health establishment. So with brushes sticking out all over—even through the opening in the roof—I drove the crew to their next job. I let them out and returned to the motel for another load, and this continued until three crews were working and the other members were training. Returning to the jobs at an agreed upon time, I was surprised to find all the jobs done and inspected. I went over the check sheets with each crew and examined the jobs themselves. All three were well done. We seemed to be improving our work posture with the new training techniques and the janitorial consultant. When we arrived at the motel, I noticed Bob walking around the parking lot with his hands outstretched. He seemed to be walking on a crack in the pavement that resembled a straight line. "Bob, what are you doing?" I queried.

"I'm keeping the balance," he replied.

"That's interesting," I responded, "would you explain that to me?"

"Well," he replied, "If I drop my right or left arm, I hear loud voices, but when both arms are extended and I walk a straight line, I don't hear the voices. So in order to keep my mental balance, I extend both arms and walk a straight line when the voices are bothering me and then they go away."

My answer was "hmmm."

As the business began to improve so did the requests for service, and soon advertisements were placed by the business manager in the paper. At this point new uniforms were purchased by the group that were quite becoming. A few days later, I asked Jack if the group had given any further thought to the type of truck they wanted and what they wanted on it. He presented me with a list of requirements and said they had also settled upon the make of the car and an agency that handled it. So without further ado, four of us got into the old station wagon and headed toward the auto agency. Jack took charge and asked to see the sales manager who eventually introduced him to a salesman. Jack and the three committee members went over their needs with the salesman and all the members agreed upon the van's accessories and the price.

Finally, the salesman turned to them and said, "All I need now is the color." The members looked at each other and began arguing. Eddie said, "I like blue," and Smitty answered that he hated blue, but loved red. And all three began to lobby for their favorite color.

The salesman became concerned and turned to me whereupon I held my hands up in the air and said, "It's their van—the color is up to them."

Each person seemed to have become a lobbyist for a particular color and the salesman stood there bewildered. Just when it appeared that there could be no resolution to the color issue, Eddie screamed, "I've got it—the perfect color. We're a janitorial business aren't we?" All the members nodded. "Then it is easy—white for purity."

"What a good idea," said Jack, and all three agreed. The salesman, shaking his head, wrote down white in the space provided on the form.

They drove the new van back to the motel. When I arrived, they were sitting in the truck laughing.

"What are you laughing about?" I inquired.

"Well," Jack answered, "we were coming back

and as we approached the viaduct on Black Street that goes over the freeway, a riderless horse came over the viaduct and cars were scrambling everywhere. Finally, the horse ran into a shopping center and someone grabbed the lead rope. A man arrived with a horse trailer and took the horse away. It didn't appear to have a scratch. As they were putting the horse in the trailer, a policeman came by and said to Eddie, "What's going on out there?"

Eddie replied, "A lot of nervousness."

The policeman nodded and drove away. We all laughed.

But getting a new van was not without its problems. A few days after the purchase I arrived at the motel to find Jack waiting for me. "Our new van is gone," he yelled.

"What happened?" I asked.

"Well," he responded, "John came to me last evening and asked if he could borrow the van to go see his brother whom he had not seen for several months. Since he had a license and had often driven trucks, I could see no reason why he should not be allowed to take it for a few hours to see a close relative. When I got up this morning the van was not here. So I called John's room and he had been gone all night. Then I called the police and they have put out an all points bulletin and that's all I know." Just then the phone rang.

"Pardon me a moment I'll go inside and get the phone," Jack said.

He soon returned with a smile on his face. "You can't imagine what happened," he laughingly said.

"No I don't suppose I can," I answered.

"Well, the police picked up John and the van just before the Nevada border. The police said John wanted to talk to me and he was furious. He said, 'I asked you if I could borrow the van to go see my brother. You said yes and now the police picked me up and said the van is reported stolen by you,' he yelled. 'Why are you going into Nevada?' I shot back, 'Well, hell, my brother lives in New Jersey,' he answered. 'You didn' tell me that,' I replied, 'I thought he lived near here.' 'Hell no, everyone knows he lives in New Jersey, stupid.' he said. Eventually he calmed down and I told him we had to have the van for our work. He said he'd turn around and come back right away. He should be here sometime tonight. We must be on different wavelengths, Jack concluded."

"Yes, I imagine you are," I responded. And I thought "who isn't."

The purchase of the new van was followed by a series of changes that seemed related to their perception of themselves as businessmen. In the next few days, training programs were established for each member. The janitorial consultant helped the crew chiefs improve their training manuals for each of the positions—crew chief, assistant chief, and worker. The members agreed to further study the manuals and learn precisely what was expected for each job—who was to bring the tools, drive the truck, and find on the map the place where the jobs were located. In addition, the business manager's responsibilities were clearly described—taking orders over the phone, newspaper advertisements, billing the customers, and so on. Driving members to their physician for emergencies and check-ups were arranged. The cook elaborated each person's overall obligation to the unit—making their beds, keeping their rooms clean, appearing on time for meals, etc. were all spelled out. And an aura of "this is our place and business" began to appear.

At this point, it appeared appropriate for me to distance myself further from the groups. I asked Jack to call a meeting of the group so that I could talk to all the members. That evening I entered the motel and was immediately greeted by all the members who were assembled in the dining room.

I opened the meeting by saying, "What I have asked to see you about this evening is the future of our relationship. First of all, you now have your own van and the business seems well underway. You don't really need me as much anymore, so I'm going to come out for a few minutes each morning and evening. If there is an emergency, call me and I'll come out immediately. Does this seem reasonable to all of you? Please feel free to speak up."

Jack replied, "I think it's great that you have

this much confidence in us . . . . Is that right or not, fellows?"

"Yes, yes, yes," several different members responded.

And with that I said "good evening" and left.

But the society was not all business and no social life. Many began going out to dinner and dances. One of the members had a particularly interesting experience. John had been a child prodigy in playing the piano. Over the years, he had developed a habit of attending the opera in San Francisco. He continued that practice in the motel. He dressed in his tuxedo and walked to the bus stop where he rode the bus to the opera house in San Francisco. One Sunday morning, I got a call from Jack who asked me if I had seen the San Francisco paper. I said, "no" and he asked me to look at it and I would have a big surprise. Since I took the paper, I opened it up and there on the front page was a picture of John and the president's daughter. The large type over the picture read "president's daughter and unidentified friend." It was startling to say the least. Later in the day, I dropped by the motel to see John and get the full story. One of the members on the grounds said John was in the dining room eating. Since John was very obese, the society's physician had placed him on a diet. When I entered the dining room, John sat there with the biggest ice cream sundae I had ever seen—many scoops of ice cream with chocolate, strawberries, whipped cream and nuts.

I said to John, "I thought Doctor Cutler had placed you on a diet?"

"He sure did," acknowledged John, "but I already ate it. I always eat my diet before my meal so I won't forget to take it."

I didn't know whether to laugh or cry, so I simply looked incredulous. After taking a few moments to recover, I asked John about the picture of him and the president's daughter.

"Yes," he responded, he had seen it."

"How did it happen?" I asked

"Well," he answered, "I arrived at the opera at the same time a limousine pulled up to the front curb. Out of it stepped this woman and she walked into the opera building with me. I saw all these people coming up to us and cameras were flashing, but I had no idea what it was all about." With that he continued to devour his sundae, and I left with what must have been a puzzle on my face.

A few days later on my evening visit with Jack, he said he wanted to spend a few minutes with me. As we sat down, he began, "We've all voted to reorganize the way we handle our business and personal problems. I wanted to see what you think of this plan. We all agreed that for many of the routine problems, there was no need for us to have everyone meet. So we decided we would have an executive committee comprised of me, Eddie the bookkeeper, Whitney the cook, and the five crew chiefs. All issues will be brought before us on weekly meetings, but if there is an emergency, we'll meet at that time. It seems foolish that we all have to meet for some simple issue like a book-keeping problem. What do you think?"

"Why don't we give it a try. If any trouble develops with the procedure, you can always call a group meeting and change the procedure. You'll never know if it works until you try. So go ahead," I replied. And so the executive committee was born.

At this point in time, the group also began to gain some positive support through their business relations. Jack walked up to me on one of my morning visits and handed me a number of papers. "What are these?" I questioned.

"Those are the results of our survey of clients," he answered.

"What do they say?" I asked.

"Read them and see how far we've come," he replied.

As I leafed through the different sheets, I saw only satisfaction with the work. "There are no complaints here," I said.

"That's what I mean," he emphasized.

"Well, it seems to me that your training programs and checking of each job have paid off for you. As my old farmer neighbor used to say to me when I worked for him as a child . . . 'You done good.'" And we both laughed—a laugh of satisfaction I might add.

Not everyone was happy though. As Jack walked away the CPA drove up. When he got out of the car he said, "I'd like to see you for a few minutes."

"Okay," I replied, "let's adjourn to the office."

"I'm going to have to resign my position with the members as their auditing service," he stated.

"Why?" I queried.

"I can't stand the slowness of the bookkeeper and some of his odd behavior," he retorted.

"Like what?" I questioned.

"Well, every now and then the bookkeeper's arm flies up in the air," he rejoined.

"So?" I responded.

"It bothers me," he continued, "and then there is that guy with the little anvil who talks to it every now and then. It just gets on my nerves and I worry. Sometimes I wonder if I'm going to get hurt. Someone might slug me," he remarked.

"Have you ever seen anyone hit here?" I asked.

"No, it's just a worry . . . these people are so different I can't stand it," he responded.

"I think perhaps you should leave if you feel that uncomfortable," I stated.

"Thank you," he said.

As he left, he told Jack he would not be back. Jack came up to me and said, "Thank God he's gone. He's been such a pain in the ass."

The next day a new CPA was hired. Several weeks later he was on the grounds when I came in for my evening visit. He came up to me grinning from ear to ear. "Boy," he spontaneously said, "I really like this group. They're so much fun to work with. You know the regular business people I work with are so well-dressed and so predictable, and so stiff. They are all worried about their jobs and making money. Most seem to have little concern for the feelings of others. But this group is different. They try to learn, and if they're a little slow they laugh but they keep trying. And they always bring me a cup of coffee and ask about my family. What it boils down to is that I like them and they like me. In fact, it's like a real vacation coming out here."

"I'm glad you like working with the members," I responded.

"Who wouldn't?" he replied.

Indeed, who wouldn't? I thought.

And the newly formed executive committee began its trial by fire. They soon found that several members weren't working up to their capacity and so they began a system of "docking" pay for those whose work was sloppy. This was not a popular decision. But these incidents of pay reduction were only the beginning of the test of the strength of the executive committee. I received an emergency call one evening from the assistant director of the executive committee asking me to come to the business office for a consultation. When I arrived I saw all the members of the committee except Jack, the chairman.

The assistant chairman, Sydney, said, "We're

really depressed this evening because Jack has begun doing some things that are not helpful to our business. We wanted to talk to you about it."

"Go ahead, I'm listening," I replied.

Sydney blurted out, "Jack has suddenly begun to yell and curse at the members. He tells us he's in charge and we have to do as he says. But worst of all, he has begun to tell customers that we are all crazy and he has lost us jobs."

"Yes," chimed in Whitney, the cook. "I remember when we first started, he made that ten thousand dollar foolish bid on a job and you overruled him . . . he got very mad and told us about it for days. He seems to be doing the same thing again. We've asked him to see you and he says 'go to hell.'"

"And so," added Smitty, "we had an executive committee meeting, which he refused to attend, and we voted him out of office. We told him he could stay as a worker, but he'd have to change his behavior. He's packing his things now . . . says he's leaving. Would you go talk to him?"

"Sure," I said.

As I headed toward his room, I saw Jack walking toward me with his two suitcases.

"I've talked to the executive committee and they say that you will not take a worker's job until things get straightened out," I remarked.

"Hell, no. I built this goddamn place. These bastards can't do anything without me," he yelled.

"That's not true. You've all done a great job so

far, but your success depends upon all members helping each other," I replied.

"Well, to hell with them and you, too. I'm leaving," he yelled.

"Remember, you can always apply for readmission," I said as he stalked out of the gate.

Well, I thought, *I hope he can make a go of it.* I watched as he disappeared in the dark and then I returned to the meeting room and told them Jack had gone. "Now you'll have to get a new chairman," I said. And then I went home.

For several weeks after that, the executive committee operated with a rotating chairman. But it soon became apparent that a new leader was emerging. He was a young crew chief who was an excellent worker and leader. His crew soon became the best crew in the business and he quickly gained the acceptance of the other crew chiefs who had been there for longer periods of time. At one of the executive committees he was asked by the members if he would consider the chairman's position and without hesitation he accepted. He immediately began supervising each crew and making suggestions about how they could improve their work. When I saw him a day later he appeared to be an executive bent upon improving the work of this small company.

His name was Lindsey and he suggested to me, "I want to run this place like I would run my own business. I assume that's okay since I was elected by the group, and they can kick me out whenever they want to. What I think would be an excellent move would be if you would place yourself on call and not come to the motel unless one of us calls you."

"That's fine with me as long as you feel free to call when you want help," I answered.

"Yes, I do and I will," he replied, "and I'm going to place all the other consultants—janitorial, legal, accounting, and the rest also on an on-call basis. I want to do this because then we are really on our own. It's like a family business which I used to run with my father. We never called anyone unless we needed their help." And so a new era of self-sufficiency was started.

A few days later, I received a call from Lindsey. "We would like for you to be here for our party at eight o'clock tonight," he said.

"I'll be there," I answered.

When I arrived at the motel and walked into the dining area, everyone turned to me and raised his glass and shouted, "Hooray, Hooray, Hooray," I chuckled and asked, "What's this all about?"

Smitty looked at me and joyfully said, "We have finished our last job with mental health professionals. Now our business is not dependent upon them for success. We have downtown buildings and other places to clean and calls are coming in all the time. We have one truck, and we're going to buy another. We're really making progress. We all love it here. It's great."

"I'm very happy for you, but one thing I don't

understand is why you're so happy to get rid of the professionals since they helped you get started by giving you jobs," I responded.

"The reason is," Smitty continued, "that they never trusted us. Let me give you an example. We used to work for Mrs. Nelson, the nurse from ward fourteen. She always found a reason to come visit us while we were working—usually three or four visits during a clean up. We knew she was checking on us like we were still in the hospital. By contrast, when we go to a job with regular people, the supervisor or owner always gives us the keys and says, 'Call me when you're done.' We never see him again until we call. What we're really celebrating is the freedom to be ourselves— to run a business like anyone else."

As I left the party I thought, *I wonder how many professionals would understand that.* And then I remembered a statement made by my training psychoanalyst that therapy is over when the patient tells the therapist to go to hell.

A few days later, on Sunday, which typically was their day off, I got a call from Eddie March, the bookkeeper. "I'd like to see you, if you could come over," he said.

"I'll be right over," I replied.

When I walked into the office, Eddie explained, "I just wanted to talk to you about Jack, he's been bothering me. It's just how sorry I am that he left because God knows he needs this place. But on the other hand, it's so difficult because its important that he leave the way he was behaving because he would have destroyed this place for everyone else. I just wanted to make sure you knew that no one here wanted Jack to leave. We all liked him very much. But we also couldn't let him destroy everything we all, including him, had created. It's a perplexing problem in all of life that one person can destroy a whole group, and yet that person actually needs the group more than anyone else."

"Yes, it is a perplexing issue," I responded. "I appreciate your telling me about how everyone feels, but I do know and understand."

"I have to get back on the books, Doc," Eddie continued. "Thanks for coming in."

"It was my pleasure," I answered, and indeed it was.

CHAPTER 7
The Enigma: Competition and Cooperation

Not long after he was elected to the chairman's position relinquished by Jack, Lindsey began insisting on better job performance by the crews and evaluated each job when it was believed completed by the crew, thus adding the dimension of perfect performance for each job. He called me one evening and asked that I meet him at the business office.

When I arrived, he said, "I suppose you have heard that I inspect each job before it can be considered finished and that some of the members are mad at me for it," he began.

"Yes, I have," I acknowledged.

"It's working," he continued. "We receive praise from almost all of our clients, so I keep telling the executive committee that we need to continue these types of inspections to keep up our good reputation at the work sites. Not all agree, but the majority do. Since we are doing so well in our janitorial business, I have had another idea—that we should expand our business by starting a landscape business. What do you think?"

"It sounds okay if the members agree, but the members also need to be trained," I answered.

Lindsey added, "We've spent a great deal of time talking about this and several of the members say that they have experience in trimming fruit orchards, so that we could begin this right away since now is the fruit trimming time."

"How do we know that the members have the skills required to trim trees?" I asked.

"I don't know. Is there any way we could check on their skills?" he asked.

"I know another psychologist whose family owned fruit orchards, and I'll ask him about it, if that's okay with you," I responded.

"Please do," he said. As I was leaving, he added, "I'll also look into training for landscaping."

When I arrived in my office, I called my friend, Don Lang. I told him what I had been told—that three group members insisted that they had extensive experience in trimming apricot, peach, pear and cherry trees.

Don said, "Tell the group I'd be willing to come out to the motel and give them a test to see if these three people know enough about trimming fruit trees so that they could go into the business. I relayed the information to the group and a date was set for Don to come and meet the group and give the members the test.

On that date, Don and I arrived on the motel grounds which were rather spacious and toward the rear of the macadam driveway were several types of fruit trees. I walked out to the fruit tree areas accompanied by Don and the three members who claimed to know how to trim fruit trees. Don turned to Ed the member closest to him and pointing to a cherry tree asked, "How would you trim this tree?"

Ed looked carefully at the tree, walked around it, and then pointing to various branches answered, "I'd cut this branch off here, and this one off here," and so on and on he went. When he was finished, Don looked at me and shook his head. I got the message that this was not the correct way to trim the tree.

He then turned to Alan and pointed to a peach tree and asked, "How would you trim this tree?" Like Ed, he pointed to many branches, and then pointing to a particular place on each branch said, "I'd trim it here." Again, Don looked at me and shook his head. Again I got the message.

Finally, he turned to Paul, and pointing to an apricot tree asked, "How would you trim this tree?" Paul looked at the tree for a moment and pointing to the bottom of the tree, he moved his hand horizontally while stating, "I'd cut this baby off right about here."

Don smiled, looked at me and said, "Well, let's

adjourn, and I'll discuss this with the Doc." As the members left, Don said firmly, "None know how to trim fruit trees, and for God's sake, don't let the last one near a tree." At that point we both laughed. Reporting back to the group, I said that Don felt they were not knowledgeable enough about tree trimming to work the orchards.

After this incident, the members seemed eager to learn how to do landscaping properly. Lindsey contacted a top level landscaping firm and they agreed to train the members. Soon three crews of three members each were trained and they began the landscape business. Lindsey insisted on inspecting each job when it was finished as he still did with the janitorial work. Both types of business became more and more prosperous. Job specialization occurred. Several persons became known for their expertise in certain types of jobs. Bob became known as the "stove man" because he was especially good at cleaning stoves. He was therefore assigned to any crew that was going to a job where a stove needed cleaning. Smitty became the business manager—assigning jobs, lining up work for each day, making out paychecks, keeping the books, answering the phone, and doing other business tasks. The society had indeed become a family-oriented business. With this impressive performance, the members considered themselves citizens contributing to the broader society. But the members were soon to receive a rude awakening.

Lindsey called me one day and asked me to come to the motel because he had some good news for me. When I arrived, he was excitedly discussing the fact that they had been hired to do the clean-up for the entire construction of a 12-story building, and in addition, the construction superintendent informed him that if they "did a good job" they would be hired to do all the clean-up work for this major construction company. The next morning, two crews got into their new van and headed toward their job. At the end of the workday, the superintendent praised them for their work and told them all how pleased he was with what they had done. This continued for two weeks. Every time I was asked to come to the motel I was told how much they liked the job and the workmen there.

A few days later, I received another call from Lindsey who asked me to come to the motel as soon as I could get there. When I arrived, the group was in the midst of a meeting and asked me to come into the room. For the first time in many days, I sensed that something very important to them had happened. All the members seemed depressed.

"Doc," Lindsey began, "we lost the construction job today, and we don't know what to do."

"What happened?" I asked.

"Well, just before we were to leave, the boss said he wanted to see me. While the crews were loading the van, I went to his office. He never looked me in the eye when I went in, so I thought that was a little strange. Then he said, 'We won't be needing your crew any more' I was shocked. 'Why not?' I asked. 'Why don't we leave it at that,' he said. 'No,' I replied, 'I want to know what we have done wrong.' 'Nothing,' he responded. 'But we're only one-tenth of the way through the job. You'll have to recruit new crews and train them.' I responded. 'I know,' he replied, 'but I have no choice . . . I suppose I might as well tell you. My boss came out here this afternoon and he was very angry. He stalked into my office and said 'What in the hell are you doing hiring a bunch of nuts from the mental hospital?' Then he told me that your company was made up of crazies from the hospital and he never wanted you to set foot on this property again. I was told to terminate your services immediately, but I decided to wait until the end of the day. 'But' I replied, 'there is nothing wrong with our work—in fact, you have told me it was excellent.' 'That's right,' he said, 'but the company policy is not to hire anyone who has now or ever has had a mental illness.' 'Goodbye,' I said, and walked away.

I looked at Lindsey and said, "What has just happened to you and the group will probably happen again. There is a lack of understanding among the public about mental illness. Many are frightened by what they read in the papers. You'll often see statements about mental patients or former mental patients in the papers. Usually the reporters state that some such person has committed a crime. What they don't say is that the number of crimes committed by people with a diagnosis of mental illness is far below the number committed by the general public on average. What the public should know, therefore, is that they are far safer with you than with those who live in their neighborhoods. But that doesn't make for good publicity. Beyond this clear discrimination against you because you have once had a mental illness diagnosis, it is wise to remember that there are other people who will not discriminate against you and, in fact, will try to help you. What it all boils down to is that when this becomes an issue, you will need to work for those who will not discriminate against you."

Lindsey then turned to me and remarked, "We voted unanimously before you came that we would never mention our mental illness to the public since they clearly can't handle it. If people know about it or ask us directly, we'll tell them, but if not we'll not make an issue of telling them. Is that okay?"

"As citizens," I replied, "you have the right to do whatever you wish as long as it's not a violation of the law."

"Well," Lindsey mused, "you really have to be careful of those "normal" nuts running around out there—they're crazier than hell. They think we're crazy, but we know they are."

With this reminder, Lindsey called a meeting

of the entire group. When they had all struggled into the room, he began, "We have again found out how mean people can be when they hear that we have all spent time in the mental hospital. Because they are crazy with fear about mental illness, we must not tell anyone that we have been in the mental hospital unless they ask. These people can't deal with it. So always be well-dressed when you go out—be sure your uniforms are clean—and speak clearly. Any questions?"

"I don't like this approach," said Smitty.

A black member, Jay then spoke up, "Lindsey is right. My grandmother always told me that the best way to avoid racism was to be better than the white kids since, like it or not, they were the majority group in our society. It's the same thing here. The public is so afraid—usually because any person who has had a mental illness and commits a crime hits the newspapers big. If the banker steals a million, it's on the back page and his lawyers soon shut it up. So it's up to us not to give people a chance to hurt us. So forget the job we lost—we'll get others. Chalk it up to discrimination pure and simple. I know about that."

There was silence in the group as Lindsey announced, "Meeting adjourned."

But all was not business and strife. Social activities were also a highlight of every day after work hours. Some of the experiences of the group members also served as a reminder that partying under the influence could result in behaviors that were hilarious but risky.

On the Fourth of July, I was sitting comfortably on the davenport at home and the phone rang. Lindsey informed me that Sam had been picked up by the local police and he'd appreciate any help I could give him and the members. Knowing that Sam had a drinking problem along with his psychiatric difficulties, I thought that he probably drank too much and was picked up inebriated. I was only partially right. Upon arriving at the jail, I introduced myself to the officer on the desk and asked for Sam.

The officer began laughing and said, "I'm glad you came—I want you to see this." I walked with him to a cell and there sat Sam wrapped in an American flag and that was all he had on.

I looked at him and asked, "Sam, what happened?"

Although clearly inebriated, I could understand him when he whispered, "I just got overwhelmed with patriotism, and then I saw this flag on a pole. I thought about America and it suddenly came to me that people are always talking about wrapping themselves in the flag. I thought that would be a wonderful patriotic gesture, so I took my clothes off and climbed the pole, took down the flag and wrapped myself in it. Then I was just walking down the street feeling very patriotic when this cop came by and picked me up. I don't understand it—it's the Fourth of July."

I paid the fine and took him back to the motel

while attempting to explain to Sam why he was picked up.

Finally, he looked at me and said, "People are always talking about being patriotic and then when you try, they put you in jail!"

Incredulous, I thought.

The executive committee became concerned about Sam's behavior and decided to be more specific about what behaviors were acceptable in and out of the society. Generally, they adopted the position that since they were continually under scrutiny that it was an offense against the whole group for any member to call attention to the society through unacceptable behavior. Accordingly, they fined Sam a day's pay and restricted him to the motel for one week after which he was on probation for a month. At the same time, they informed him that they knew he was trying to express his patriotism but that he would have to do it in more socially acceptable ways in the future.

But such behaviors were not reserved only for after work hour adventures. Occasionally they occurred on the job as this work experience shows.

One crew was working on the landscape of a beautiful home located in a wealthy neighborhood. Around one o'clock, a party began at the house next door. Many people in their swimming suits had collected at the pool bar area. The crew chief later reported that a crew member, Wally, asked if he could use the van for a few minutes to go back to the motel. The crew chief gave Wally permission and the crew members continued to work. The crew chief said after about an hour it occurred to him that Wally had not returned. About that time the crew took a break and sat on the grass looking at the party next door. Suddenly one of the members gasped, "There's Wally."

"Where?" asked the crew chief.

"There at the bar in his swimming suit," the astonished member replied.

"My God," said the crew chief, "It really is him."

All members looked and gasped and then broke into uproarious laughter.

"Well," said the crew chief shaking his head, "you've got to hand it to him—he is creative."

Near the end of the work day, Wally showed up with the van, dressed in his swimming suit and telling all that he had been to a party and had a ball. Needless to say, Wally immediately was put on probation with the loss of one week's pay. Even so, the crew chief couldn't tell that story without laughing.

While events like this were hilarious and somewhat devious, they did not effect the excellent reputation that the group enjoyed with its neighbors. While I was leaving the motel one evening after Lindsey had summoned me for a work discussion, I was met at the entry to the motel by a person who introduced himself as a neighbor.

"Do you have anything to do with this group?" he asked.

"Yes, I responded, "I'm one of their consultants."

He continued, "I just want you to know how much this group means to the neighborhood. This motel was the center of a prostitution and drug ring prior to their moving in and late night parties—yelling and screaming—were the order of the day. Many of us were afraid for our children. Drug taking was rampant. Now we have some stability. These people work hard. When asked, they help their neighbors. It is an excellent group, and we're sincerely happy to have them here."

"That's very kind of you," I rejoined, "I'll tell them the next time I come out and thanks for telling me." *What a considerate neighbor*, I thought as I left for home.

And their reputation for helpfulness was reinforced that very evening. Lindsey called me later in the evening. When I answered the phone, he excitedly said, "Doc, we just stopped a robbery at the service station next door. I didn't want to call you so late, but I thought you ought to know since we gave your name to the police. Three of us were planning tomorrow's work when we heard some shouting next door. Smitty left us and soon came back saying there is a robbery going on in the service station. I just saw two men with masks and guns holding up John (the attendant). I said 'Smitty, you call the police and Eddie and I will try to help John.' When we got to the station and were still in the dark I yelled that we had guns and were coming after them. They started to run, but the police arrived and grabbed them. John wasn't hurt, so we were very happy."

"Do you want me to come over?" I asked.

"No," he replied, "we're doing fine. I gave the police your name in case they needed to verify what I told them about our group."

With this event, their reputation took a giant leap forward with the neighbors. They had become the neighborhood protectors. As John the service station attendant told me later, "When you need them, you can count on them." I wondered what their skeptics would say to that.

But all was not completely without conflict within the organization. One of the best crews began to show sloppy work habits and Lindsey became concerned. He called in a work consultant who advised him to put the group in a retraining program until they had regained their excellence in job performance. Lindsey called me and asked me what I thought of this plan. Lindsey said, "They'll bitch like hell and tell me they can already do the work, so what in the hell am I training them for?"

"I'll check into this procedure and get back to you," I answered. That afternoon I met with a friend of mine who was in charge of work crews for a national organization and I asked him about retraining.

"Yes," he said, "we often use this technique with our crews. Even our best crews need retraining once in a while. Rather than argue with them, we simply put them in retraining and tell them that as soon as their performance is up to what we know they can do, they will be returned to their regular work setting. They will bitch, but they will also improve their performance."

I relayed this information to Lindsey who immediately implemented this plan. And so, a new retraining procedure became part of the business operation.

With their improved prestige in the neighborhood and their business refinements, the number of jobs they had increased dramatically. And these business pressures began to take their toll as the Executive Committee became more and more responsive to their business success. The Committee members were crew chiefs and they began to pressure their work groups to do more work and to do it more efficiently. Lindsey, who declared himself a first rate capitalist, insisted on better and faster performance by the work crews.

As the workload increased and the profits of the business continued to escalate, the governing body of crew chiefs became more and more interested in increasing profits. At one of their meetings, they decided to demand increased productivity and they then called a general meeting of all the members to tell them of the new work rules. At the meeting Lindsey told the workers they would have to increase their productivity. Those who did not want to do so should leave the organization in order to give other more interested people who would help them increase the business profits a chance to join the organization. Soon after the meeting I received a phone call from Jim Smith, one of the marginal workers, asking me to meet with him and his colleagues at the motel.

When I entered the room Jim looked at me and said, "Thanks for coming. All of us here have helped develop this small society and business. We've been told that if we don't increase our productivity we should leave. This is not only unfair, it humiliates us. We have been so proud of our role in developing the society that we are all stunned. The question is, what can we do?"

"Is this not a democratic society?" I asked.

"Yes," he replied.

"Did you not establish by vote the executive committee?" I continued.

"Yes," he replied.

"Do you not outnumber the crew chiefs?" I stated.

"Yes," he replied.

"Oh, I see," piped up Chris, "Why don't we call a general meeting and vote to abolish the executive committee. We'll replace it with an open meeting where all members can attend and vote. In this way we can vote down any policy we think is unfair. In fact, we could kick them out if we wanted to."

"We don't want to do that," Jim replied. "They

are good at running this place. Once they know that we have the numbers and can replace them, they'll settle down and we can all work together as we've done so far. And it's worked for all of us."

"Well, Doc, I guess that's all we needed to know—that we had the power to run this place," said Jim.

The next day the meeting was called and the workers demanded that all meetings be open in the future and all issues be subjected to vote. But as time passed, the workers quit attending the meetings and the crew chiefs took over again by default.

This led me to reflect upon what is a common happening in democratic societies. The workers here, as in many societies, had handed over the operation of the society to an executive committee of their members. The committee became more and more powerful as time went on and since they made the most income from the group's work, they decided to make rules that could eliminate many of the original members who had put them in power. Now it became necessary for the workers to arise and take back the society from a handful of their own members who had become so fascinated by the possibility of becoming rich that they lost all concern for the persons who elected them to power in the first instance. But after the uprising, the revolutionaries lost interest and a few powerful leaders took over again. Since this occurs over and over again in democratic societies, it reminded me of the Frenchman's statement, "The more things change, the more they remain the same."

CHAPTER 8
Citizenship Achieved

The research with its five years of information gathering was nearing an end and this meant that the group might need some help in planning its members' future. Preliminary research results showed the group had achieved a much better community adjustment than those persons who had gone to other community programs.

While I had constantly discussed this day with the group since its beginning four years ago, it nonetheless was an anxiety-provoking moment for both me and the group members. In the original plan I had thought that at this time I would get some local mental health agency to provide some consultation when and if it was needed. Consequently, I contacted several agencies that I thought could and would be helpful. Imagine my surprise when each agency contacted said that they were not interested because their professional staff only prescribed medication and saw patients in their offices during work hours. The common answer was that money would need to be deposited with the agency and the members would have to become mental patients again regardless of their level of adjustment. With this information, I approached Dr. Cutler, their physician for the past four years.

After we exchanged greetings I said, "Walter, I can't imagine how such a successful program can be turned down by the local professionals. After all, they could build on it and expand their services as well as using the advice and consultation of both of us and the members themselves. It seems such a natural thing to do."

"Oh, I understand," he responded. "They want total control of the treatment money and above all, they don't want to change the professional role of doing everything in their office. This would demand that they find business and other types of consultants and that they would try to help people in real life situations which would require changing their practices. Maintaining their domination and the notion that 'the patient comes to us, we don't go to the patient' is a well-entrenched norm of operating programs in the community. The main interest is maintaining the bureaucracy and control of professional roles and money. It's that simple."

"Well, obviously I'm going to have to rethink this entire matter and discuss it with the members," I replied.

Later that same day I called Lindsey. "I'll need to see the entire group as soon as I can, "I said.

"Fine, I"ll arrange that," he replied. And so, two days later I met with the entire group. When everyone was seated I began by saying, "As all of you will probably remember, this is a five-year project that is terminating. Accordingly, the persons who have let us use the motel want it back and the payment for consultants will end. I'd like to hear what your plans are and how we can carry them out."

"We have already thought that through, and we have a plan," Lindsey said.

"What is it?" I asked.

The business manager, Smitty, quickly spoke up. "We have been saving our money, and we have enough now to make a down payment on two houses. In fact, we knew this day was coming, so we have already talked to several real estate agents. A few want to leave and return to their families or start a new career, but most of us want to stay together. We have our own business, and we believe we can make it. Oh, one thing, Doc, we'd appreciate it if you would let us do this completely on our own. We'll see if Dr. Cutler wants to continue to see us as his private patients, but otherwise, we want nothing to do with the mental health establishment."

"Would it be possible for me to see you after a few months to see how you are doing?" I asked. "I really need to get this information for the research. You have been very kind so far, especially filling out all the forms I've given you, and also letting me use your records."

"Would you mind leaving the room for a few minutes while we discuss this?" Smitty asked.

"Not at all," I answered.

As I sat waiting for their response, I thought, *They've come a long way. They have actually attained full citizenship.*

Then Smitty appeared and stated, "We've decided that you can visit us twice—at six months, and again at one year if you will promise not to bother us after that. It's not that we don't appreciate what you've done—we do—but at the same time, we want to run our own program from now on. No consultations unless they're what we want. We can't be dependent on you forever."

"I appreciate what you have said. In three months our lease runs out and you'll have to move," I reminded them.

"Fine, I'll tell the group," Smitty remarked. And the final movement toward citizenship had begun.

Within a few weeks the members had made a down payment on two houses and prepared to move into their own homes. I was surprised to find that they had accumulated several thousand dollars from their work and that they still had a "nest egg" when they moved into their houses. But before their move a new problem arose. I was called one evening by Lindsey who wanted to see me as soon as possible. I immediately drove to the motel and entered the business office. Lindsey was there, and after greeting me, he appeared worried as he said, "I wanted you to be the first one to know that I'm getting married. My wife works and her company is giving me a job so I'll have to tell the members that they'll need to elect a new chairman of the executive committee. In many ways, I hate to do it, but I think it's in my best interests to move on."

I responded, "I appreciate your telling me. You have been more than fair to the group. Many of the work and business procedures that you developed will live on with the group."

"I hope so," he responded, "but if they need me I'll come and help. I'm going to leave my phone number, and I'll be available."

"I'm sure they'll appreciate that," I said.

Two days later I received a call from Whitney who asked me to come out and see him. As I drove onto the grounds he was standing there and greeted me.

"Well, I'm the new chairman," he announced. "I know that you probably wonder how I can manage a group like this since I've usually been in charge of the kitchen. But I was the one they all wanted so I'm it. What do you think?"

"The main issue is—do you think you can handle the job? You've been here since the group started, so you're familiar with all the people and procedures," I responded.

"Well, I think I can. I'll never know if I don't try." And so the Whitney era began.

The move to their new homes began a few weeks later. By now they had three trucks and a mountain of landscaping and janitorial equipment, and so the move took two days. At this juncture an event occurred that was to shape their relationships with their neighbors for the next several months.

I arrived on the grounds just as the last van load was about to leave. I saw Whitney behind the wheel and I went up to the side of the van and said, "You're just about moved out. How does it feel to leave home?"

We both laughed and then he got out of the truck and said, "The move has been fine, and we're all happy except for one thing."

"What's that?" I asked.

Whitney looked very puzzled and then said, "It's Bob and the new neighbors."

"What happened?" I further inquired.

Whitney grinned and said, "You know Bob, he's always kind of funny, no matter what he does. He is always a kind of 'tongue-in-cheek' guy. Well, anyway, as we were moving in a couple of neighbors came over and started asking us all kinds of questions. We all thought it was rather strange, but we continued our work anyway. Finally, one neighbor said, 'Where are your wives?' I could tell Bob was getting more and more antsy. He answered 'We don't have any—why should we, we're just a bunch of nuts from the mental hospital anyway.' Let me tell you, those folks left the area in a hurry and none of them have been back—in fact, they go across the street so they don't have to speak to us. After they all left, I turned to Bob and said 'thanks.'"

"What did Bob say to you?" I queried.

"He said, 'They ain't bothering us anymore, are they?' Then the whole group laughed. I guess in a way it's about all we could do."

"Good luck in the community," I said. And we both laughed.

Six months later my agreed upon time to visit the members arrived. I went to the house where Whitney lived and rang the doorbell. It was late in the evening and he came to the door. I was surprised to see a drink dispensing machine in the living room although otherwise it was much the same as any other home.

"I noticed you were looking at the cold drink machine," Whitney said.

"Yes," I answered, "I have never seen one placed in a living room before."

"Well," he said, "when we come home from work, we're all thirsty and some of the fellows drink several cold cans of pop or beer. When we moved, we soon found that this created a traffic jam in the kitchen and several members felt that one or two of the members were taking more than their fair share of drinks. So we bought a quarter machine and installed it where there was the quickest access to it after work—furthermore, each drink costs a quarter, so that each person pays for his own drinks."

Hmmm . . . I thought . . . *very creative.*

I then asked Whitney what was the end result of Bob's statement about the "nuts" from the mental hospital.

Whitney replied, "There is sort of a coolness between our group and the neighbors. They're not outwardly mean to us—they just ignore us. They obviously don't want to talk with us. I've also had a problem of getting the members to draw the blinds when they undress. You know, we were somewhat isolated on the motel grounds, and we paid little attention to having neighbors because the motel was surrounded by the high fence. So no one bothered to close their blinds there. Everyone continued that practice here until one night our phone rang and the voice said, 'I'm one of your neighbors, and you people are undressing in front of the upstairs windows. Would you please pull the blinds.' They wouldn't tell me who they were. I rushed upstairs and told everyone to close their blinds, and if they did leave them open not to undress in front of them. We're already in enough trouble with the neighbors. Smitty, who was in the room replied, 'Yeah, I guess they can't stand the human body. Well, what else is new.'"

"Did that end the problem?" I asked.

"I think so since I have never heard a word about it again." He went on, "There are some other differences here compared with the time we spent in the motel. The biggest is that we have tailored the operations of the household tasks and outside work to each person's interests. As you know, Bob never did like to work in the big buildings, and since most of our janitorial work is located there now, we asked him what he would like to do. He said he would like to keep up the house and yard and also work on the landscape crews if extra help was needed. We voted on this, and it was approved unanimously, since most of the fellows don't like to make their beds and do dishes anyway. It has worked out real well. And our social life has improved. Many of the fellows have girlfriends and go out several times a week. Of course Bob, Eddie and Joe don't go out much. You will probably remember that they always were homebodies. They watch a lot of TV. Our work remains about the same. We have all we can do and have had to turn down several new jobs because we don't have enough people. We're also starting to put away money for retirement. We've continued to give shares in the business to the workers so that our members continue to increase their ownership in the company. All in all we're doing very well."

"What about the member's symptoms. Are they better or worse?" I inquired.

He continued, "Some members are better and some about the same. Everyone seems to be at least holding their own. No sudden changes. Oh, we have arguments now and then like any group, but we have managed to handle our problems.

When these things happen, we try to get together and talk things out like we did in the motel. It works well for us. And we also have continued to see Dr. Cutler when we need to see him. He's been a great help. We've seen him for so long it's like seeing a relative when we have to go. No one goes unless he asks us to come in or we feel bad. That way we don't take up too much of his time."

"Is there anything you'd like to tell me before I leave?" I asked.

"No, I think we've pretty much covered everything that needs to be discussed. Thanks for coming," he responded.

"I'll see you in six months," I said as I left the house.

I had made arrangements earlier to see Dr. Cutler to get his views about their adjustment. We exchanged greetings as I entered his office. "What's your opinion? How are they doing?" I asked.

"Very well," he responded. "They seem much more relaxed than they were in the motel, and it shows in a reduction in symptoms. Not a single one has had a negative reaction. And they watch each other's medication like they did in the motel. If anything, they are better now. I sure wish I could get some of my other patients to take their medication as seriously as this group does. I'm impressed. I would like them to come in a little more cleaned up than they do, but after all, they are workers and they often come in from their jobs in their work uniforms. Of course, many of my other patients come from their offices or are retired so this difference should be expected. Generally, they are doing fine."

"Thanks for your time, Walter. I'll see you in about six months for a final meeting on their adjustment." I thought about what a rag-tag group they had originally been and how well they were adjusting now. I felt very proud of them.

At the end of twelve months, I returned to the group's home for the last time. Whitney greeted me at the door and asked me if I wanted a cold drink from the dispenser at the end of the living room. I had forgotten about this distinguishing feature and I said, "Sure."

"What kind?" he asked.

"Anything is okay." With that, he handed me a lemonade. "Thank you," I said, "and what's new?"

He added, "Our business is still doing well. In fact, the members continue their retirement fund for themselves in addition to their social security. We now have health insurance along with our other insurances—house, car, liability, and so on. Smitty and John have been able to do fine without their medication and we've grown to appreciate Dr. Cutler more and more. But the biggest change is with our neighbors. Several of them have become friendly and these folks now treat us as neighbors and friends."

"To what do you attribute that?" I asked.

He continued, "Well, one of the women met us

in our yard one evening and asked Smitty what he knew about schizophrenia. He said quite a bit, but so did several people in the house. She said her brother had been recently diagnosed as schizophrenic and that none of his friends and some family members didn't want to see him anymore. She had him over and he seemed okay to her, but a little irascible. So anyway, we told her all we knew and recommended she see Dr. Cutler for advice. She sent her brother to see him. So now her family likes us and she told another friend who has a sick sister. We also talked to her and sent her to see Dr. Cutler. Now it seems we are— we are now accepted."

I replied, "It sounds like you are becoming the neighborhood mental health consultants. If you enjoy it, more power to you. I'm especially glad that you feel free to send them to see Dr. Cutler."

"Well, since you've been gone, he's become more than a doctor to us—he's our friend," Whitney replied.

"Is there anything else I can do for you and the group. Remember, according to our agreement this is my last visit," I added.

"No, I don't think so," Whitney responded. And so I walked out the door for the very last time. I felt sad and happy at the same time. Happy for them and everything they had taught me, and sad like the teacher who had worked with students whom he liked very much.

And there was yet the last visit with Dr. Walter

Cutler. The next day I saw Dr. Cutler in his office. "What do you think now after they've had a year on their own?" I asked.

"There is no question in my thinking that they have accomplished every goal they established for themselves. Their health is good. In the past six months, two more have gotten off medication. Their symptoms, while not wholly gone, have improved. All in all, the outcomes, as far as I know them, are excellent. From my perspective, you can leave with very positive feelings," he replied.

"That sounds like all the other information I have," I responded. "I'll send you a copy of the data analyses when they're printed, and you can see if you and I are right. I certainly appreciate all you have done for them, as I know they do. Is there anything else you think I should know?"

"Yes," he said, "I told Whitney that I would drop off Jake's medication on my way home a few days ago. I went up to the door and Whitney invited me in. It turned out that they were having snacks and drinks for the neighbors who began drifting in as soon as I arrived. I handed Jake his medication and he asked me to stay for a snack and a drink. Since I was on my way home, I said 'sure.' Everyone was dressed up and so I wasn't out of place. After a while, one of the neighbors came up to me and said, 'Boy, I never would have guessed that you were mentally ill.' I responded, 'It goes with the territory.'

We both laughed and then I said, "You know,

when they first moved into the motel, they decided if they put suits on no one would believe they were mentally ill. One thing you can say, Walter, is that they knew more about it than most people." And we both laughed as I left his office.

By the time the last visit was over, I began to get the results of the comparisons of the group members with their counterparts who had gone to the other community programs. As I studied the statistical analyses and their accompanying time graphs, the day-to-day living and working advantages of the member-owned business and living arrangements became more and more pronounced. Because the results were so positive in favor of the small society, I found myself checking the results over and over again. One day, as I was looking at the results for what seemed like an endless number of times, my old friend, Bob Morse walked into my office.

"Well, what does the data say?" he asked.

"It is rather astounding," I said. And, I continued, "In every single measure of adjustment we took, the small group society is not just ahead, but overwhelmingly so. Let me list a few for you. In a four-year period, only five percent of the small society's members returned to the hospital contrasted with over 75% of those in the other community programs — all of the group members, of course, left the hospital, but one-third of their comparison group never got out of the hospital in those four years. And the value of having their own business is clearly seen in this graph." I held up the graph for Bob to see where all the group members worked at least two-thirds of their time while in the community but those in the regular community programs were generally unemployed. I continued "Now look at this graph of costs. At no point did the group program cost more than one-third of the regular program's costs, and of course, they have now become self-supporting, paying taxes and the like. And equally or more important the morale and happiness of the group members is better than their counterparts as shown in this graph."

Bob replied, "It's time to show these research results to those who can implement this program on a national scale. I'll call my friends in Washington and make an appointment for you to see them as soon as possible. This is great news."

CHAPTER 9
Facing the Controlling Bureaucracy

In my scientific training, I had learned that important research evidence showing the superiority of a new program would usually result in its adoption. With this and my clinical background, it seemed just a simple step to provide the scientific information of the group's success to the proper authorities. After all, this new community program helped patients become contributing citizens, they were happier, the staff was pleased, and all of this was done at little cost with the society eventually gaining because the former patients were tax-paying citizens. Armed with this information in graphical and statistical form I contacted the mental health officials that Bob Morse knew in Washington and I asked for an audience to whom I could present this research information. The audience was granted and I soon found myself heading to Washington certain that this convincing evidence would result in national adoption of this new patient-oriented program.

Upon arrival I entered a large building which was rather sparsely furnished and was immediately directed to the top floor. Upon leaving the elevator, I was surprised to see the plush surroundings especially when contrasted with what an incoming citizen would see when entering the building. I was led into a large meeting room with highly polished tables and comfortable furniture like one might find in any private industry's CEO headquarters. A number of professional persons filed in and the show began. I displayed all the charts clearly showing the treatment and economic advantages of the new program contrasted with those in existence. After a two-hour presentation and a question and answer period, the chairperson dismissed the meeting. As the people filed out, all of them gave me their personal congratulations for a research well done.

The chairperson then said to me, "That was an excellent presentation of a well done research."

"Thank you," I said, "What's next?"

"What do you mean?" he replied.

"Well, when does this program begin on a national basis?" I asked.

"I have no idea—research is separate from treatment—each has its own budget. It may never be used by anyone," he responded.

"You mean to tell me that problem-oriented

research is done just for the knowledge one gains—that it is often paid for by the government, and therefore the public, but may never be used by the people for whom it is intended?" I queried.

"That's right . . . it's separate, it has nothing to do with treatment," he continued.

"But in my training I was taught that research was the very foundation for new treatment programs," I asserted.

"Then your training was wrong. For example, suppose the professionals don't want it. With your program, they'd have to get out of their offices and go into a different kind of training. Even if your results are correct, the people who determine treatment are not the patients, they are the doctors. With the kind of results you have, if it were a new drug or surgical technique, the patient could sue for malpractice if treatment were denied. But not in the behavioral sciences, since they're so shaky anyway," he declared.

As I turned away from him I thought—*my training was wrong when it comes to changing the mental health bureaucracy. Now I've got to find out how to do that so the patients can have this program.* And so, a new adventure started.

A few days after I returned to my office, I received a phone call from a doctor in another state.

"I just heard from a friend of mine about your new program. Is it really that successful or are you fudging the data?" he asked.

"No, it is very successful. I'll send you a copy

of the study. Tell me what you think of it." I replied.

A few days later he called back.

"I can't believe it, but if it's that good, I want it here. We have 7,500 patients and many have been in the hospital for years. Can someone come down and help us start it?" he asked.

"I'll see what we can do," I said.

Later that same day, I talked to one of my colleagues and he said, "I'll go help them get started."

When Dale arrived, he found a large, old mental hospital with a very interested staff—particularly the nurse. Within a few days, they had designed and implemented the required role changes that permitted the patients to become more involved in decisions that allowed them to take more responsibility for their own lives both in and outside the hospital. In a matter of weeks, problem-solving groups were organized and moved into community residences. At the same time, they organized their own businesses.

After returning from the hospital, Dale kept in constant contact with the hospital personnel. He burst into my office one day and said, "This program really works. Patients are in the community and being treated as citizens within weeks. And like our research data suggests, both the hospital staff and the group members are happy with the new program. But one problem remains. That is the difficulty that the staff has in letting the group alone to solve its problems. They feel like they are failures if the group falls short in some problem-solving areas. Its the same problems we went through in the experiment. I'm in the process of developing more tools to help them surmount their feeling of failure if the group doesn't do well for awhile. As we learned earlier, this is part of the process."

"Yes," I responded, "They have to learn that a child can't learn to walk unless it falls down. Falling is not a failure, just a part of the learning process."

With this success, it seemed that a way of implementing this new program aimed at group member autonomy had finally begun. But in truth the difficulties had just started. As time went on, other professionals contacted me and asked about implementing the program. As these new calls came in, it became apparent that the persons who called were those who believed that the mental health program in their area needed to be changed. In a sense, these were the change agents who had become disenchanted with the mental health system and wanted to try something that was based upon research evidence that showed it was beneficial for the patients. As each person tried to start the program s/he met one obstacle after another. This was most clearly reflected in a meeting that I was invited to by a group who had started the community program.

One of the members of the staff that met with me said, "You mentioned in your speech the many obstacles that one faces in trying to do anything new in a bureaucracy. Well, I appreciate that because we have had one hell of a time here because the members have had a mental illness diagnoses." He handed me a newspaper that told how the members of the community were trying to keep the ex-patients from moving into their new house. Then he said, "It's amazing how every time a person who has had mental illness is involved in a crime, it makes the headlines, but when a well-known community family member commits a crime, it's usually on the back page in little print. Yet the public doesn't seem to know that there are far fewer crimes committed by the mentally ill than by typical members of the community. In any event, the paper is finally coming to the rescue and I'm proud of them for that."

The staff member continued, "A person that I know is a state legislator and has a son who is mentally ill. He told me that his colleagues were going to cut the funding on community programs, and we'd be among them." And then he added, "I told the chairman of that committee that I would vote against agricultural funding for his county if he voted to cut mental health expenditures. The chairman soon became a staunch supporter of funding these programs and received the other legislator's vote for agriculture appropriations for his county." The young man shook his head and continued, "It seems that everything has become so politicized nowadays that political power becomes the main determinant of what services are provided to those who need them. Money seems to grease the wheels for all decisions. It seems like money has become our God, and if one is to get funding for a program that helps others, it has nothing to do with the merits of the program. This is very sad for our society."

"Yes," I replied, "It certainly is, and this should be a concern of every citizen. But on the positive side," I continued, "we have now started a number of small societies and their businesses despite these bureaucratic power problems. What this indicates to me is that changes can be made in the bureaucracy but great persistence and motivation are required to do so. Maybe that's why this program is only being started where some highly motivated adopters are involved."

Further evidence for this notion continued to come in through letters and telephone calls from those interested in the self-governing society. One particular phone call remains in my memory as if it were yesterday. A mental health professional called me one day shortly after the aforementioned visit. I answered the phone and the person was crying.

"What's wrong?" I asked.

She responded, "I'm sorry for crying, but we have had a terribly catastrophe here and I thought I'd call and ask your advice."

"I'll do the best I can," I responded.

"Well," she continued, "we followed your plan

and developed an excellent program here with mentally ill women who began a sewing business. We have done extremely well with the business and the women were very happy. Last night a fire started in the house for reasons we still don't know about. I received a phone call from one of the members telling me to get right over to the house because of the fire and to tell me they had notified the police. When I got there all the residents were out of the house but it burned to the ground and they lost everything. Some neighbors were there standing around who didn't know me and one turned to me and said, 'Well, that's what they get. You bring a bunch of crazies into a house and of course they'll burn it down. I never wanted them here in the first place and I'm glad they'll be gone.' I asked him, 'How do you know they started the fire?' He answered, 'Well, anyone knows that, that's what they always do.' Then I asked him, 'What about the mayor's house that burned down two months ago?' He responded, 'Probably one of these people started it.' As I began helping the frightened residents get into my van with their few belongings, I thought how difficult this must be trying to live in an area with the feelings expressed by this resident."

"Have you found housing for the residents?" I asked.

"Yes," she responded, "we're all moved into a new place and we're doing okay. Still a little frightened, but okay."

Recalling my experience with the first society I said, "It may take some time of being good citizens before your new neighbors will accept you, and some probably never will. Our experience is that those who do accept you—even though gradually—will become your support system eventually. You might also try to interact with the neighbors as one society I know about has done. They have a periodic open house once every three or four months and invite the neighbors. It has worked out quite well for those who have tried this approach. But it is most important to recognize that some people cannot or will not accept anything new. For this group, standing up for your rights as citizens may be the only way. In such cases, you may need legal advice. In any event, without the residents and your own hard work, I can assure you nothing will be done. But let me put you in touch with the members of the group who holds these open houses for the neighbors every three or four months and who are now viewed by the neighbors as friends. In this way they have slowly become looked upon as part of the neighborhood."

"I'll try that and let you know what effects these open houses have upon the members and the neighbors," she answered.

A few weeks later, she called and said, "We just held our first open house and it went very well. Many of the neighbors came and seemed to enjoy themselves. So thanks for the tip. On another matter, the fire chief just revealed that the cause of the fire that destroyed our first home was a gas leak in the basement. It was published in the local paper and I certainly hope that our former suspicious neighbors read their papers yesterday. One of our group members said when she was reading the paper, 'Why do they say we're paranoid. Maybe they ought to look at themselves.'"

As time went on and new groups began organizing, it became more and more clear that not only did the residents have to deal with their own problems and those of their other group members but also those of the community and the mental health bureaucracy. This was no more dramatically illustrated than in a state where several local citizens had started several new small societies. The citizens were ecstatic about the return to citizenship status of the society's members—greater employment, improved behavior and attitudes at a dramatic reduction in cost. Using their successes along with our original research data showing the success of these societies contrasted with other programs, they approached the state mental health authorities in an attempt to get some state funding for creating new societies and making them available to other mentally ill volunteers.

While visiting these societies, the mental health professional who had helped start them informed me of this attempt and added, "We had no success at all. The mental health director told us that their program for these people was to put them on medication and that was being done." He continued, "I responded that our members were also on prescribed medication but that, in addition, they were employed and happy about their lives. And the reduction in cost was about one-third of the original cost and eventually it was nothing, in fact, the members were paying their own way which not only made them feel good but also helped the taxpayers. The director answered, "There's nothing I can do about it. Their doctor decides what's best for them and that's it."

He turned to me and asked, "What can we do?"

I responded, "Everyone has to recognize that mental health treatment is just as much a political and economic problem as it is a curative one. What I suggest is that you and your friends enter the political arena. Take your evidence to the politicians since it is clear that the mental health bureaucracy will do nothing about it and, in fact, typically has a greater interest in maintaining and protecting the income of its members and their lobbyists than it does in the happiness and well-being of these low status persons."

"Okay," he said, "we will."

A few months later I received a telephone call from him.

"We did it," he yelled.

"What did you do?" I asked.

"We got funding for the program. You were

right, it was a political battle. But finally, we got some help from a number of professionals, relatives and friends and together we got some money from the mental health establishment to start other societies," he continued.

"That's fine," I responded, "but remember this will be an on-going battle at every budget session. Special interest groups always come back since their interest is typically money and power. They don't like to adopt new programs—particularly those that empower the mentally ill and by so doing give them the ultimate voice in their own lives. Good luck. Keep me informed."

Similar problems continued to emerge with interested persons in other states. While reflecting upon the unwillingness of some groups to help others, particularly when it involved those without political and economic power, a member approached me while I was visiting a society one day. He said, "Is this the land of the brave and the home of the free, or what?" he asked.

"Yes, it is," I replied, "but it is also the home of the essential narcissists and the power hungry."

As more and more people heard about the member-led small society and its success, it became increasingly clear that barriers of all types arose in order to keep rehabilitation money flowing in the direction of the traditional professional mental health workers and their programs. A very clear indication of this occurred when I was invited by an interested person to present the research results to a group of professionals. When the presentation ended one psychiatrist raised his hand and said, "We've had group programs like this for years. I don't see what you're so excited about."

I answered, "Who makes the decisions in the programs you're describing?"

"The psychiatrist, of course," he responded.

After the meeting was over, another psychiatrist caught up with me as I walked down the hall and said, "Of course, Dr. Watson sees no difference because he can't comprehend that mentally ill persons can make good decisions—but you're lucky—you don't have to work with him. Keep up the good work. There are some of us who think you're on the right track." And this became the theme of the adoption of the new program. Some people were willing to change and others were not. And indeed, it was often a matter of economic and political control.

This was again emphasized when I arrived home the next day. When I entered my office, I found a note asking me to call a Mrs. Kelly in a distant state. I called and introduced myself and she said, "I read about the member-owned business and society in your recent book. I am a psychiatric nurse and I took all of the information to the next staff meeting. I was informed in no uncertain terms that this staff was not going to turn over any decisions to groups of mental patients—that they should stay in their patient roles and do what they were told. I then asked if there was any interest in empowering programs, and was told 'no.' So I resigned from the staff after deciding to establish my own member-operated society. Several churches are helping us get started with contributions, bake sales and the like. I've found a large number of members who are interested in a program like this. Many have had relatives in mental health care for years and they want to try something new. So with their help, we've rented a home and we have started a new business. Everyone is really excited. Relatives have said their mentally ill kin have never looked so good. And we all know that if we don't change the system, no one will."

"You have repeated what we have found across this country. Keep your own records and show your colleagues. One day they may change their position. Good luck and thanks for the call," I responded.

I thought then of the sociologist who had studied social change most of his professional life and had stated, "The best way to change a social system is to build one next door that more adequately meets the needs of the public."

The general nature of this resistance to change became more and more evident to me each day. After a presentation at a large clinic, a young psychologist asked to see me about a problem he was having. "My name is Curtis Wall" he said, "and I have run into a serious problem with a group of young people. I have read about your program, and I am trying to use the decision-making principles with this group. They are adolescents who are from well-to-do families. They have run away from home because they believe their parents do not love them. They say all their parents do is work and play golf at the country club. They're never home and never have been. These children are now in high school. They have dropped out of school and have congregated under a bridge. I go down there every night helping them organize their group. The police have come and taken them home over and over again and they simply run away again. Some of the group has started back to school and the rest say they will. They're looking for a house and some place to stay, and I think I will be able to get them housing soon. I've talked to the parents and their attitude is 'good riddance.' They are not going to help these people. We have been making some progress and I think they'll soon all be back in school and have housing, although I doubt they'll have much of a relationship with their families. Eventually I think they will become a family through helping each other. But the current bigger problem is that the head of my agency has told me that I can't see them anymore to help them develop this family relationship."

"Why not?" I asked

"He says we do psychotherapy in our offices and that I have no business visiting them under a bridge. That I am a professional and not a social change agent. What do you think I should do?"

"I can't answer that for you," I replied.

He responded, "It seems like every time I try to do something new, I run into the system. I thought we were supposed to be creative in trying to help people."

"So did I," I replied, "So did I."

As time went on, it became evident that some of those working within the bureaucracy also wanted to adopt the new program. An assistant director of a state's mental health program called me one day and asked if we could meet to discuss the possibility of his state adopting the society as part of the state's mental health effort. He decided to come and see me after our talk. A few days later I met with him in my office. When he walked in he said, "My name is Bert Mellon and I'm very pleased to meet you."

"Have a seat," I responded, pointing to a vacant chair. "How can I help you?" I asked.

He continued, "When I read about your research, I was very impressed, and so I got it into our funding as one of the mental health programs in the budget that was passed by the state legislature. It was approved, and when I looked for the money to start a small society a few months later, I found that it had already been spent—but not on this program—on one where the bulk of the money went to professionals, not to developing small businesses owned and operated by the patients. So this year I again asked for the money and I immediately had it placed in my account. We will start the program now. You might say I beat them to the draw."

"Isn't that illegal—getting money for one program and using it for another?" I asked.

"Not in our state," he said. "Getting the money is one thing, but spending it is quite another. After the mental health division gets the money, they have ways of spending it for their favorite programs which are usually those endorsed by the mental health establishment. Empowering the mentally ill has not been one of their favorite concerns, but spending money for programs that have many professional personnel is. Since I am a strong supporter of the mentally ill, I have been able to keep some start-up funds for your program this time."

"You're a brave man," I replied.

"No, just someone more interested in the mentally ill than in the politics of people who run the establishment," he added.

Our discussion continued for most of the day, and when Bert left, he was ready to start the program on a state-wide basis. And indeed he did. I was again struck by the fact that the adopters of programs that put the mental patient first were drawn from every walk of life. It was clearly a personal matter having to do with the degree to which each professional was concerned about the welfare of these unfortunate persons—some a great deal, some somewhat, some a little and some not at all. And it brought to mind Einstein's puzzlement about why it was that so many people had such a motivation to try to dominate others. Should Aristotle return to earth today, he might wonder, as he did during his lifetime, why societies still had such social inequities. But whatever the reason, it appears from my experiences that certain members of society will continuously against all odds try to correct these inequities and it is to them that all societies owe their greatest debt.